THE CRAFT
OF
POLITICAL
ANALYSIS
FOR
DIPLOMATS

ALSO BY RAYMOND F. SMITH

Negotiating with the Soviets (Indiana University Press, 1989)

ADST-DACOR DIPLOMATS AND DIPLOMACY SERIES
Series Editor: Margery Boichel Thompson

Since 1776, extraordinary men and women have represented the United States abroad under all sorts of circumstances. What they did and how and why they did it remain little known to their compatriots. In 1995 the Association for Diplomatic Studies and Training (ADST) and Diplomatic and Consular Officers, Retired, Inc. (DACOR) created the Diplomats and Diplomacy book series to increase public knowledge and appreciation of the involvement of American diplomats in world history. The series seeks to demystify diplomacy by telling the story of those who have conducted U.S. foreign relations, as they lived, influenced, and reported them. Raymond F. Smith's *The Craft of Political Analysis for Diplomats*, the forty-eighth volume in the series, illuminates the professionalism the best diplomats employ in serving their country.

OTHER TITLES IN THE SERIES

HERMAN J. COHEN, *Intervening in Africa: Superpower Peacemaking in a Troubled Continent*
BRANDON GROVE, *Behind Embassy Walls: The Life and Times of an American Diplomat*
PARKER T. HART, *Saudi Arabia and the United States: Birth of a Security Partnership*
EDMUND J. HULL, *High-Value Target: Countering al Qaeda in Yemen*
CAMERON R. HUME, *Mission to Algiers: Diplomacy by Engagement*
KEMPTON JENKINS, *Cold War Saga*
DENNIS KUX, *The United States and Pakistan, 1947–2000: Disenchanted Allies*
TERRY McNAMARA, *Escape with Honor: My Last Hours in Vietnam*
WILLIAM B. MILAM, *Bangladesh and Pakistan: Flirting with Failure in Muslim South Asia*
ROBERT H. MILLER, *Vietnam and Beyond: A Diplomat's Cold War Education*
RONALD E. NEUMANN, *The Other War: Winning and Losing in Afghanistan*
RICHARD B. PARKER, *Uncle Sam in Barbary: A Diplomatic History*
RALPH PEZZULLO, *Plunging into Haiti: Clinton, Aristide, and the Defeat of Diplomacy*
YALE RICHMOND, *Practicing Public Diplomacy: A Cold War Odyssey*
HOWARD B. SCHAFFER, *The Limits of Influence: America's Role in Kashmir*
HOWARD R. SIMPSON, *Bush Hat, Black Tie: Adventures of a Foreign Service Officer*
JAMES STEPHENSON, *Losing the Golden Hour: An Insider's View of Iraq's Reconstruction*
ULRICH STRAUS, *The Anguish of Surrender: Japanese POWs of World War II*

THE CRAFT
OF
POLITICAL
ANALYSIS
FOR
DIPLOMATS

RAYMOND F. SMITH

An ADST-DACOR Diplomats and Diplomacy Book

Potomac Books
Washington, D.C.

Library of Congress Cataloging-in-Publication Data

Smith, Raymond F., 1941–
    The craft of political analysis for diplomats / Raymond F. Smith. — 1st ed.
        p. cm. — (Adst-dacor diplomats and diplomacy series)
    Includes bibliographical references and index.
    ISBN 978-1-59797-729-6 (paperback: alk. paper)
    ISBN 978-1-59797-730-2 (electronic edition)
    1. Diplomacy—Methodology. 2. Political science—Methodology. 3. Diplomats—In-service training. I. Title.
    JZ1305.S62 2011
    353.1'3270973—dc22

                                                                            2011013946

Printed in the United States of America on acid-free paper that meets the American National Standards Institute Z39-48 Standard.

Potomac Books
22841 Quicksilver Drive
Dulles, Virginia 20166

First Edition

10 9 8 7 6 5 4 3 2 1

*To the men and women of the United States Foreign Service
and to their counterparts in other countries*

CONTENTS

ACKNOWLEDGMENTS

I began this book for two reasons. First, I had some ideas on doing political analysis as a diplomat that I wanted to share with others. I spent a lot of my diplomatic career either doing political analysis or overseeing it, and I think that is the aspect of the profession that I was best at. Second, I think the public impression of the Foreign Service in particular and the diplomatic profession in general is rather negative. I hoped that providing some actual examples of Foreign Service political reporting, along with some background about how it is done, would contribute to a better understanding of at least this aspect of Foreign Service work. I have dedicated this book to the men and women of the United States Foreign Service, as well as to their colleagues in other countries, because they are trying to make things better and because their efforts are often unappreciated.

An abbreviated version of some of the ideas in this book, presented from the perspective of intelligence reform, appeared in the journal *Intelligence and National Security* (volume 24, December 2009) under the title "Is It a Pearl or a Kidney Stone? Intelligence Reform and Embassy Reporting, from Moscow to Baghdad."

I had the benefit of comments and suggestions on an earlier draft from several former Foreign Service officers: Richard Combs, Mark Foulon, Jack Zetkulic, and an anonymous reader from the Association for Diplomatic Studies and Training. They helped to improve both the content and the tone of the final manuscript, although I am entirely responsible for the flaws that remain. I would like to thank ADST for accepting my manuscript into its publishing program and its editor, Margery Boichel

Thompson, for her editorial suggestions, her help in placing this work with Potomac Books, and her positive outlook. My brother, Joseph Smith, who is a State Department information management officer, helped update my understanding of the Department's communication and distribution system and policies.

My wife, Ann Miller, is a good friend and a great partner. She makes my life better in many ways.

GLOSSARY OF COMMON STATE DEPARTMENT TERMS

Diplomacy, like most professions, has its share of acronyms and shorthand terms. Here are some of the common ones used by Department of State and Foreign Service personnel and in this book.

CIA—Central Intelligence Agency.

Congen—consul general.

DAS—deputy assistant secretary. However, the shorthand "AS" is never used to refer to assistant secretaries, probably because unless the speaker carefully controls sibilance, unfortunate connotations may ensue. "A/S" is often substituted in writing.

DCM—deputy chief of mission. The number-two-ranked person at an embassy. He or she is in charge of the embassy—with the title "chargé d'affaires ad interim," or "a.i."—when the ambassador is out of the country. The common shorthand for this is "chargé."

DIA—Defense Intelligence Agency.

Emboff—embassy officer.

EXDIS—exclusive or executive distribution. This is a distribution designator placed on a document to restrict who may see it. It serves other uses as well, which are discussed in the text.

IC—intelligence community.

IMF—International Monetary Fund.

NODIS—no distribution. Another, and even more restrictive distribution designator. Despite the terminology, these documents are distributed.

NSA—National Security Agency.

NSC—National Security Council.

Polcouns—political counselor.

Poloff—political officer at an embassy. Other offices will have their own shorthand, as in "Econoff."

Seventh Floor—senior State Department officials (under secretary and higher). Derives from the fact that the office of the secretary of state is on the seventh floor of the main State Department building in Washington. The term has also come to connote policy approval, as in "the Seventh Floor has signed off on this."

In addition, each bureau in the department has its own shorthand designation, as in "EUR" for the European Bureau and "INR" for the Bureau of Intelligence and Research. Combining a bureau indicator with a position indicator, such as "EUR A/S," allows accurate designation of both the position and the individual occupying it, without the bother of attaching an actual person's name. However, no way has yet been found to apply such designations when more than one person occupies the position, as in "EUR DAS," and last names are pressed into service in such cases.

CHAPTER ONE

WHAT IS POLITICAL ANALYSIS
AND WHY IS IT A CRAFT?

This book is intended primarily for practitioners and prospective practitioners of political analysis and for those with a specific interest in how the craft is practiced. It is not intended to be a philosophical, historical, or etymological treatise. Nevertheless, some definitional work is necessary so that both author and reader share a common understanding of the content to follow and its boundaries.

For the purposes of this book, politics has to do with social relations involving authority or power. It could be argued that all, or virtually all, social relations involve authority or power, but that would be to define politics so broadly as to rob the term of any analytical utility for present purposes. Family politics, office politics, and gender politics may all be legitimate objects of inquiry, but they are not what we are concerned with here. The "polis" was an ancient Greek city-state, a geographically defined entity governed by a body that existed to regulate the affairs of its constituents. We shall be concerned with politics primarily as they concern authority or power relations within and between those regulating bodies that we know as governments, and between them and the societies they are regulating.

Analysis is an endeavor that involves separating an intellectual or material whole into its constituent parts for individual study, studying such constituent parts and their interrelationships in making up a whole, and/or preparing a spoken or written presentation of such a study.[1] In political analysis, then, we may be deconstructing governmental or other entities concerned with power or authority so as to better understand how particular parts work, or, conversely, we may be looking at the entity as a whole with a view toward understanding how it affects, and is affected by, its constituent parts.

1

To summarize, we shall think of political analysis as the attempt to convey an understanding of how authority and power relations operate and evolve within and between governments and between government and society.

I believe it is more useful to think of political analysis as craft than as science or art. Having a craft essentially means having a skill at making or doing something. Often, in the past, one would have apprenticed before being accepted into membership in a trade association or guild, thereby becoming recognized as a craftsman. A craft is not a science, although it benefits from and partakes of science because it contains elements that can be taught and mastered. It is not art, because it is essentially utilitarian rather than aesthetic, although the work of the finest craftsmen may rise to the level of art. At its best, it combines the intellectual rigor of science with the aesthetic sensibility of art. The subject matter of political analysis does not easily lend itself to the rigorous application of the scientific method. Opportunities for controlled experimentation are rare. History at the social level and experience at the individual level are generally thought of as the best teachers. But the lessons they teach are subject to widely varying interpretations. Art emphasizes the subjective. It is the imposition of one's personal aesthetic sensibility on "objective" reality. Political analysis that relies too heavily on one's own aesthetic sensibility—or, to put it another way, on a personal worldview—is no longer reliable. It does not listen. It marshals facts to support a preordained conclusion. Yet that insight, that artistic sensibility that makes the leap from incomplete information to the correct conclusion, that creates a new understanding of a complex reality, distinguishes the brilliant craftsman from the journeyman.

In democratic societies, political analysis is fair game for everyone. Private opinions are, generally, welcome in the public arena, and a variety of media are not only available, but protected as means for expressing them. It is worth remembering that this was not always so. The salons and coffeehouses of the Enlightenment, and the publications prepared and circulated within them, created the first post-Roman public venues for political discourse. Within these venues, the exchange of political ideas was no longer confined to the nobility and their satraps, but could include the artistic, literary, and commercial classes.

It remains true, however, that although Everyman may be a political analyst, not everyone engages in the craft of political analysis. The craft is practiced by members of particular professions: academics, journalists, diplomats, and perhaps even politicians. What differs them from Everyman? Not unimportantly, they are paid for practicing this craft. They have been appointed, selected, elected, or otherwise placed in a position that allows them to exchange their political analyses for money. This is not necessarily to say that they practice their craft entirely, or even mostly, for money. But in market societies, there tends to be a presumption of some particular skill or talent at that for which one is paid.

All practitioners of the craft of political analysis work on the same subject matter. Beyond that, however, their differences may well outweigh their commonalities. Broadly speaking, they use different analytical techniques, have different vocabularies, address different audiences, are concerned with different time frames, use different vehicles to convey their work, have different objectives. They face different criteria for success and different pressures to succeed. They are competitors, rivals, and, only occasionally, collaborators. They recognize one another as practitioners of the same craft but often find little in common as they go about their work.

What characterizes diplomatic political analysis? This is a subject for discussion at greater depth in succeeding chapters, but a brief overview at this point may be in order. The journalist and the academic write for publication, for the public. Anyone may see their work. Lack of interest is the only bar. The diplomat's work is generally classified for security reasons. It reaches only those who have the appropriate security clearances and, among them, only those who have the "need to know," although developments since September 11, 2001, have begun to change these criteria[2] and the unauthorized release of some 250,000 State Department reporting cables in 2010 (the so-called "WikiLeaks" release) may change them again. The small target audience and the security classification should encourage candor but do not necessarily do so, for reasons to which we shall return.

The diplomat works with a specific primary objective in mind: to protect and promote his country's interests.[3] While it is always nice if the interests of one's own country coincide with the interests of all mankind, the diplomat's job is to promote his country's interests, not those of all mankind. His analytical work should reflect this objective. Of course, defining those interests is a complex subject in itself, a combination inter alia of personal experience and outlook, historical experience and tradition, and the views of his country's leaders. However arrived at, this definition will influence all aspects of his work, including the choice of subjects on which he will report and the kind of information he will collect and include. The journalist and the academic, ideally at least, have different objectives. The journalist reports on what he sees. He does not participate in it. The academic seeks a scientist's dispassionate understanding of what unfolds. While it would be naïve to assert that institutional interests or personal views or ambitions do not play a role in the worlds of journalism and academe, there remains in the code of these professions an impulse towards a stance of objectivity. The diplomat has no such pretense of objectivity. He is a participant as well as an observer. He has a point of view—if you like, an axe to grind. This is not to say that his analytical efforts should not be as accurate as he can make them. It is difficult to see how one can advance one's country's interests by providing inaccurate information, although, paradoxically, the diplomat does face pressure at times to do exactly that (another subject to which we shall return). But, in the end, all of the diplomat's efforts have to include a response to the question, what does this mean for my country? If it means nothing, he should be spending his limited time and energy on something else. That is not a question that the academic or the journalist is required to address.

Political analysis is both an oral and a written craft. We will deal with both, although greater stress will be on the written craft, since that is the form in which embassies usually convey their analyses, and the primary focus of this book is on the diplomatic post abroad as the *producer* of political analysis and the ministry at home as the *consumer*. Some of the same skill sets are involved, but it is rare for a person to be superior both as a written analyst and as an oral briefer. It is worth thinking about the reasons why this is so. In written analysis, most of the information received by the audience comes from the actual words used. Grammar and style should be so seamlessly integrated with content as to be unnoticed. Poor grammar or inappropriate style distract from the information conveyed. One writer has referred to situations in which most meaning is conveyed by the actual words used as "low affect" activities.[4] The oral briefing, by contrast, is a high-affect activity in that the recipient uses a much wider range of environmental cues to infer meaning from the presentation: physical attributes, body language, tone of voice, etc. Persuasiveness in the written document depends much more on marshalling intellectual arguments than it does in the oral briefing. At the extreme, the oral briefer may be so compelling that he persuades not by what he says, but by how he says it. Form triumphs over content.

Let me offer an example from my personal experience. After I had been at one of my first foreign posts for about a year, the new embassy economic counselor arrived, a person widely recognized to be a rising star in our diplomatic service. A month or so later, he presented a briefing to embassy staff on the economic situation and prospects of our host country. He made a brilliant and utterly persuasive presentation, which concluded that the immediate prospects for the country's economy were poor. A couple of years later, having departed the country but remembering that presentation and curious about how the economy had actually done, I checked. The economy had grown quite respectably, about 6–7 percent annually, over the ensuing two years. If the prognostications in that brilliant and utterly persuasive presentation had been wrong, how much of the rest of the analysis was also wrong? There was no way to check, of course, because there was no written document. In any case, no one remembered the content of the presentation. What everyone remembered was that it was brilliant.

Oral briefings that build around a presentation tool such as PowerPoint are widely used. The PowerPoint emphasis on ticks, bullets, and shorthand can change the underlying analysis, as well as its presentation. On the one hand, such tools allow key points to be reinforced visually. On the other, emphasis may be placed on a few eye-catching phrases rather than on the substance of the analysis that accompanies them.

This should not be interpreted to mean that written analysis is "better" than oral analysis. They are simply different. Written analysis has the advantages of engaging the intellect more fully and providing a record that can be referred to more easily. Oral analysis may offer greater opportunities to persuade and influence, along with greater risk that the persuasiveness may come not from what is said, but from how it is said. A variety of technological developments, discussed in the final chapter, suggest that oral briefings may be in the ascendancy, even highly sensitive briefings between embassy staffs abroad and their counterparts and superiors at home.

Mid-level foreign affairs officials read a lot. Most senior officials rely more heavily on oral presentations than on written briefs. The young diplomatic political analyst who aspires to high position and influence will have to master written analysis early in his career and hone oral briefing skills as he begins to climb through the ranks.

CHAPTER TWO

THE OBJECTIVES OF DIPLOMATIC POLITICAL ANALYSIS

The objectives of diplomatic political analysis are to inform, to explain, or to influence. The terms "reporting" and "analysis" are often used interchangeably. Embassy political reporting is a generic term that may include one or more functions of reporting (informing), analysis or prediction (explaining), or recommendations (influence). They are distinguishable and should be distinguished because they have different content, different objectives, and, often, different audiences.

The U.S. intelligence community is bifurcated into operations and analytical branches. The operations branch comprises what we think of when we think of the CIA— the spies, the spooks, James Bond, et al. Its job is to use clandestine means to collect information and transmit that information to Washington along with an evaluation of its accuracy and reliability. This is reporting, not analysis. The Station (the CIA's office at an embassy) reports what it receives. It generally limits its interpretation and analysis of the information, although it may comment on it. Most analysis is done in Washington by the analytical branch, which wants just the facts. By putting together facts from a variety of sources and methods, it produces an interpretation, or analysis, of what they mean.[1]

The State Department is organized differently. Its operations and analytical efforts are not so clearly differentiated. One of its divisions, the Bureau of Intelligence and Research (INR), is considered to be part of the intelligence community and devotes itself entirely to analytical efforts. The secretary's Policy Planning Staff also has primarily analytical functions, although how it is used varies more widely as senior department officials come and go. Much of the rest of the department, including its geographic, economic, and functional bureaus, performs both operational and analytical tasks. A country desk within a geographic bureau may, for example, on the same day be dealing with the problem of a diplomat from country X caught shoplifting (it happens!), and providing senior department officials its evaluation of whether a threatened mineworkers' strike in country X could destabilize the regime in power.

Embassies also work both sides of the operational and analytical fence. Embassy officers may on the same day be organizing a visit to the United States of a group of host-country journalists or assisting a congressional delegation that is in the country, and drafting cables for Washington readers about a variety of developments in the country. An embassy cable may solely report, or analyze, or predict, although it is more likely to be some combination thereof. The distinction is simple enough in principle, but it is a distinction worth noting because, as indicated above, of the differences in content, objectives, and audience.

EXAMPLE: MINERS' STRIKE IN COUNTRY X
A reporting cable, simply comprising factual statements, provides information to interested Washington readers. At a minimum, these readers will presumably include the country desk officer or officers and members of the intelligence community responsible for following developments in that particular country. The country desk will decide whether any higher-level officials in the department need to be made aware of the information. The intelligence community will incorporate the information into its analyses of what is happening in the country.

The "Simplified Flow of Embassy Reporting" chart gives a simple picture of how a typical embassy reporting cable is distributed to offices and agencies in Washington. Which offices and agencies will receive a particular cable is a function of a number of variables. The key ones, to which we will return later, are subject matter, security classification, and distribution restrictions. Each office and agency will have its own

Simplified Flow of Embassy Reporting

| Embassy | → | Country Desk | | Other State Dept. Offices | Other Foreign Affairs Agencies | National Security Council |

Geographic Bureau

Seventh Floor

criteria—some automated, some not—for determining how embassy reports are distributed, both horizontally and vertically.

Let us use a miners' strike in country X as an example. An embassy officer arrives at work in the morning, picks up the local paper, and reads that there may be a walkout by miners. Assuming he has the right connections and is on top of his game, he arranges to see the head of the mineworkers' union and the chief of staff to the minister of the interior. He gets a cable out that evening that says:

> Speaking to emboff[2] in his office at union headquarters, miners' union chief _____ said that his workers will walk off their jobs at noon tomorrow unless they get a 10% pay increase effective immediately. The chief of staff at the Ministry of the Interior subsequently told emboff that there will be a substantial police presence at the mines to ensure that those who want to continue to work are able to do so.

This is straightforward, factual embassy reporting. It deals with the "who, what, when, and where" of the situation and tells Washington readers what the embassy has learned about newspaper reports that a strike is imminent. A cable analyzing this situation might include the information above, as well as the following:

> Local union leaders are behind this strike threat, seeing it as an opportunity to challenge the central union leadership. The miners' union chief has little choice except to go along or risk losing his position. The Ministry of the Interior sees an opportunity to break this powerful union and intends to use its forces to support company efforts to bring in replacement workers.

This analysis provides context for its readers about the forces at work, about the real objectives of the various players and about the underlying power struggles at the heart of this supposedly bread-and-butter strike. It deals specifically with the "why" question. The following commentary is more predictive and attempts to address the "what does it all mean" and "why is it important" questions:

> We consider the probability of violence during this strike to be high. The miners are likely to resist attempts to bring in replacement workers, and the police appear to be under orders to use force in support of those attempts. Sympathy strikes by other unions in response to the violence are likely. If leaders of other unions perceive

this as an attempt to weaken the labor movement by destroying the miners' union, a general strike is possible. A general strike lasting longer than a week would seriously damage the economy and could topple the government.

Each of these cables serves a useful function alone, but this is a situation in which the whole is greater than the sum of its parts. Submitted as one document, this would be a rather decent embassy analysis of a potentially significant event in country X. Often, the analytical aspects of a cable are separated from the factual aspects and submitted as a final "Embassy Comments" paragraph or section. Despite the fact that the combined document is obviously more satisfactory, there are any number of reasons why the documents might be sent separately. Often, they boil down in the end to time. For example, the head of the political section may be prepared to submit the initial, factual reporting cable on his own but may be reluctant to transmit the analytical and/or predictive sections without the input or concurrence of the deputy chief of mission or the ambassador. However, they may be tied up at a social function where they cannot be interrupted. Even if they could be reached, the analytical and predictive elements of the cable are not the kinds of things one would normally discuss by telephone, even in a friendly country. The political section head decides, therefore, to transmit the factual report immediately and to save the other elements for discussion at his meeting with the ambassador in the morning.

Further, analytical and predictive efforts take more time to draft and are subject to greater differences of opinion. After all, no one can argue with the embassy officer about what the miners' union head and the Interior Ministry chief of staff told him. There can, however, be considerable disagreement about what it all means and what the likely outcome will be. This is a subject, for example, on which the embassy's economic section is likely to have views that should be solicited and taken into account. It takes time to find language that satisfies these differing views, particularly if one wants to avoid an end result that is so homogenized as to be trivial.

The "Simplified Embassy Structure" chart gives a basic view of how a typical political officer's report will travel through the embassy structure for review, clearance, and approval. Each of the boxes represents a location where changes in the report may be requested or required.

The reader may have noted that I described this as a "rather decent" analysis. This is not faint praise, but neither is it an encomium. The factual information provided is good as far as it goes, but it is certainly not complete. There are significant players in

Simplified Embassy Structure

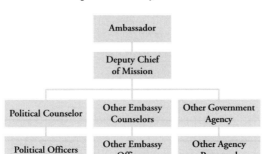

this drama who have not been heard from, including the director of the mine and other labor leaders. There may be other significant issues to consider. For example, how does the miners' 10 percent pay increase demand compare with recent raises obtained by other significant unions, and how would this affect potential support from other unions? The cable does not address what these developments mean for the home country's interests, nor does it make recommendations for steps the home country should take to deal with these developments.

It is easy enough to sit at one's desk at leisure and dissect the weaknesses of any analytical effort. The practitioner seldom has that leisure. He must not allow the best to become the enemy of the good. This strike starts at noon tomorrow. He has to balance completeness against timeliness. He also has to judge on the fly how significant these developments are, both for country X and for the interests of his own country. His personal time and energy are limited. The embassy's collective time and energy is limited. Developments that may lead to the fall of a government obviously merit substantial time and energy. If the same developments, however, are likely to lead only to a change in miners' union leadership, they take a lesser priority.

Diplomatic political analysis does not have to explicitly discuss how particular developments will affect the home country's interests. In fact, most political analysis does not. In many cases, the author will assume that he and his readers have a sufficient common understanding of his country's interests that any explicit discussion would be superfluous. This is not surprising. Both are, presumably, foreign policy experts, as well as specialists in the domestic politics of country X, its relations with the home country, and the home country's policies toward it. In other cases, the developments in question may warrant a report but are unlikely to have a significant impact on the home country's interests. A few developments (for example, a change in government) obviously warrant an explicit statement of how it will affect the home country's interests. Most do not.

Recommendations are an explicit means to seek to influence policy. But explicit recommendations are the exception rather than the rule in diplomatic political analysis. There are a number of reasons for this, beginning, in the U.S. system at least, with the distinction between political appointees and career civil servants. The president and the vice president are the only persons in the entire foreign policy apparatus of the executive branch who have been elected. The president and his senior appointees, most chosen with the advice and consent of the Senate, make the foreign policy decisions, legitimated by electoral and constitutional processes. Career civil servants, including the country's diplomats (in the United States, generally Foreign Service officers), carry out the policy. Nearly everyone at an embassy abroad, at least below the ambassadorial level, is a career civil servant in one form or another.

Political appointees vary greatly in their appreciation of unsolicited foreign policy advice and recommendations from career personnel. A wide variety of factors, many likely not known to the political analyst in the field, may come into play in determining how recommendations are perceived at home. They can include, to name just a few: the personal disposition of the reader; whether the recommendations accord with or oppose his own policy outlook; the public profile of the issue; the level of expertise in the capital on the issue. Unless they have been specifically requested, it is best for an embassy to assume that its policy recommendations fall into the category of well meant but unsolicited advice. This does not mean that an embassy should hesitate to provide its views, but it also needs to keep its audience and its own limitations in mind. An embassy may be in the best position to "see" what is happening in its host country, but it is not well situated to appreciate the range of political, economic, legal, and practical constraints on policymakers in its own home capital. Recommendations that run counter to the prevailing view at home need to be made sparingly and phrased judiciously or the "well meant" appellation can easily change to "ill-intended," which negates the chance that the recommendations will be taken seriously and may also bring with it unattractive career implications. A recipient of the Director General's Award for Analysis (to be discussed further in chapter 7) offered the following comment on this subject:

> The most serious obstacle to effective embassy reporting over the past few years has been the decline of truly candid analysis and the pervasive sense among political officers overseas that their analytical judgments are unwelcome in Washington,

especially when it calls into question the conventional wisdom or the administration's pre-conceived foreign policy in a particular area.[3]

The ambassador, as the president's Senate-approved personal appointee, has more leeway to offer policy advice than the embassy as a whole. Washington readers will assume that any policy recommendation made in an embassy dispatch has been approved by the ambassador, but those are not the same as the ambassador's personal recommendations, made face to face or in a dispatch explicitly labeled as such. Paradoxically, but for obvious reasons, the 30 percent or so of ambassadors who are political appointees rather than career officials often feel freer to offer policy advice than their (generally far more knowledgeable) career counterparts.

EXAMPLE: MOSCOW, 1988

Embassy policy recommendations are more often implicit in the subject matter on which the embassy reports than in the content of the reports. For example, when I arrived in Moscow in 1988 to head the embassy's political section, there were high-ranking officials in Washington who continued to believe that Soviet general secretary Mikhail Gorbachev's reform steps were superficial and aimed at creating a more efficient system, but one that would continue to be confrontational. In other words, if Gorbachev succeeded, we would be facing an equally antithetical but more capable opponent. This view had obvious policy implications. At the embassy, we saw the beginning of meaningful reforms that, if continued, would change the way the Soviet Union related to the rest of the world. The relaxation of controls on the media and on information flow was particularly important. Washington saw the return to Moscow from exile of nuclear physicist and political dissident Andrei Sakharov as a significant step, which it was in terms of removing an irritant in U.S.-Soviet relations. But in itself that would not have indicated significant change in Soviet internal politics. Dissidents had returned from exile before and would again. The significant sign of change was that, after his return, Sakharov was allowed an uncensored opportunity to speak on Soviet television. The totalitarian control of information that had been the practice in the Soviet Union for many decades was being relaxed.

Later, we watched a TV commentator on the 9 pm news program, which may have been the most widely watched news show in the country and was considered the authoritative voice of the Communist leadership, visit a small food market in Helsinki, Finland. He showed his viewers the variety of fruits and vegetables available, remarked that it was only one of many such markets in Helsinki, and asked why a greater variety of produce could be found here in this small market in this small country than anywhere in Moscow. It is difficult to convey the revolutionary change this represented. Suffice it to say that the show would not have been aired even a year before, and those involved with producing it would have, at best, lost their jobs—and quite possibly have gone to jail.

Explicit policy recommendations would have been superfluous, perhaps counter-productive, as we reported on each of these events. The events, our reports, and our analyses spoke for themselves in policy terms. Of course, no single cable, no single event could demonstrate conclusively, in this case or in any other, the potential impact of the processes we were witnessing. Rather, our reports on events as they occurred, supple-mented periodically by more in-depth analytical looks, sought to create a cumulative picture. Did this change any minds in Washington? Perhaps the fairest thing to say is that they contributed to a climate in which minds changed. As we look at the tools of diplomatic political analysis in chapters 5 and 6, we will try to see in a more general way how fundamental aspects of one's worldview come to be changed.

The diplomatic political analyst can use a variety of methods to influence who reads his dispatches. We will discuss these in subsequent chapters. Next, however, we need to look more carefully at who the analyst's potential audience is and the impact that has on what he writes and how he writes it.

CHAPTER THREE

THE AUDIENCE

Diplomatic political analysis can be an existential experience, done for the good of your soul and transmitted into the ether without any particular expectation that it will ever land on someone's desk. I served for several years as the only political officer at the U.S. Embassy in Ivory Coast, then a stable, peaceful, relatively prosperous West African country that had made a lot of good political and economic choices since becoming independent. Our desk officer at the State Department had responsibility for several other countries in the region as well, all of which were politically unstable, economic basket cases. She was smart and hard-working, but there were only so many hours in her day. One of her countries, traditionally unfriendly to the United States, had recently begun to make positive overtures, but its people were on the verge of starvation. In another of her countries, the pro-American ruling class had just been overthrown by an army corporal of unknown political leanings and questionable sobriety who had walked into the presidential mansion one night, shot the president, and announced that he was the new ruler. It would have been truly naïve to expect a wide readership for my political dispatches, admirable as I considered them to be, although they would probably have been read in the State Department's Bureau of Intelligence and Research (INR). Also, the more fully staffed geographic offices at the CIA and the Defense Intelligence Agency (DIA) might have had someone available to read them. Nevertheless, there are both personal (because it is good for you) and professional (because it is your responsibility) reasons to produce the best work of which you are capable.[1]

By contrast, my previous assignment had been as one of nine members of the political section at the U.S. Embassy in Moscow. We had a guaranteed audience with an inexhaustible appetite for our work. We will use this audience for Moscow reporting as the basis for our discussion, understanding that readership will vary proportionately with a country's size and strategic or economic importance, and inversely with its level of stability. It behooves the drafter of an embassy dispatch to keep in mind both who his audience is and what its members want, since different elements of the audience vary greatly in the amount and kind of information they are prepared to absorb. By keeping the target group in mind as he prepares dispatches, he can make intelligent decisions on style, content, completeness, and timeliness that increase the chances his work will have an impact. The ideal dispatch is complete, accurate, correctly predictive, and timely.[2] Much of the craft of diplomatic political analysis lies in reconciling this ideal with the limitations of everyday life.

Let us begin with a reality check. Only on the rarest of occasions will your audience include the president. The chances that he will ever see the actual text of an embassy dispatch are slim at best, in part because of the audience you can actually aspire to reach. Washington contains serried rank upon serried rank of government workers whose raison d'être is to receive information, interpret it, whittle it down into manageable size, and funnel it upward. The volume of this information is immense. For example, in 1990, Embassy Moscow transmitted about 3,600 cables per month. While most of them obviously involved routine administrative matters rather than political analysis, the sheer volume of information coming into Washington can be overwhelming. When I was not sending in those dispatches from abroad, I was at the Washington end taking part in the receiving, interpreting, whittling, and funneling. We once had a president, who shall go unnamed (at least by me), who received his foreign policy information on note cards. I know this because a high-ranking National Security Council (NSC) aide stopped by the Soviet desk where I was working and told us so. He said that at the end of the day whatever we sent him for the president was going to be put onto a note card. We could either do our own editing down to note card size, or he would do it for us.

This may be an extreme example, but it is well worth remembering because it vividly illustrates a crucial difference between the audiences for diplomatic political analyses and those for academic or journalistic analyses. In academia, if quality is equal, more is better. Completeness is a higher value than conciseness. Thoroughness is a higher value than timeliness. The journalist would rather see more of his words in print than fewer. He may suspect that his editor lives by the motto "all the news that fits we print" rather than by "all the news that's fit to print," but that is not his view.

THE COUNTRY DESK

The most consistently attentive and responsive audience for embassy dispatches should be, and normally is, the State Department's geographic bureau and, more specifically, the country desk within that bureau. A country desk can be anything from an office comprising dozens of foreign and civil service personnel, to an individual whose "desk" includes up to three or four countries. The country desk is responsible for managing day-to-day relations with a specific country (or countries) and funneling upward information or issues that require higher-level attention. It maintains contact with the appropriate foreign embassies in the capital. Despite the fact that embassies abroad and country desks at home are staffed by persons with similar backgrounds, interests, and expertise, it is not unusual for them to get out of synch with one another. Personal contact through regular visits back and forth or through informal exchanges is normally the best way to ease any tensions that may develop. Desk officers tend to deal better with, and grant greater respect to, the differing outlooks of embassy officers they know and like than the views expressed by some nameless and faceless "emboff" they suspect may be more in touch with the political sensitivities of his host country than the political realities and policy directions of his own. (For similar reasons, the embassy analyst should take advantage of opportunities for personal contact with other elements of his audience, particularly in the intelligence community.)

The country desk is the default audience for embassy dispatches. If you do not have another audience specifically in mind when you prepare a dispatch, you are writing it for the country desk. The country desk is the embassy's voice in Washington, although it also speaks for itself. The desk officer is the person you count on to ensure that embassy views get a fair hearing in the capital. The desk officer's own audience, however, is much closer at hand: his office director, geographic bureau deputy assistant secretary or assistant secretary, and, more rarely, someone higher up than that. If your reporting priorities differ from those of the persons he is reporting to, the desk officer is going to be attuned to theirs, not yours. To put it simply, the desk officer wants to be the best-informed person in the capital on the country for which he is responsible. He wants to be able to respond to any question or tasking from higher up in a way that demonstrates his mastery. He values information and analysis from the embassy that enables him to respond well to, or even anticipate, questions from his own audience. One of the most common issues the desk officer will deal with if your country is getting media attention is the request for press guidance.

COMPLETE OR TIMELY? THE DAILY PRESS BRIEFING

On issues that are getting significant public attention, much of the morning activity at the NSC and the State Department revolves around preparing for the daily noon press briefing. The headlines in the morning newspapers and the lead stories on major television networks tend to set the agenda for these briefings. The press expects the administration to present an authoritative statement of the government's position on these developments. It follows, then, that if an embassy wants its interpretation of a given event reflected in the administration's position, it has to get that interpretation in early enough for it to be considered by those preparing documents for the noon press briefing. As a practical matter, this means that an embassy dispatch must be in circulation in Washington when the business day begins. Delaying a dispatch to collect additional information or to prepare a more thorough analysis risks making it irrelevant *if* the Washington audience for the dispatch is the officials who are preparing the administration's response to the event that day. By the next day, the chances are that they will be preparing responses to other events, very possibly in other areas of the world, and will pay no attention to what the embassy has said about yesterday's news. The drafting officer at post needs also to keep in mind that putting his report in a form that enables the desk officer to do a quick "cut and paste" from the embassy dispatch adds to the likelihood the embassy's view will appear in the administration's press statement, as well as, incidentally, earning the gratitude of a harried desk officer rushing to get press guidance drafted and cleared.

There are also self-serving motives for providing timely input in these circumstances. This is when decision makers in the administration are likely to ask what the embassy's view is. If there is no embassy view to present, the embassy has missed an opportunity. Not only that, it leads influential people in Washington to begin to think of the embassy as slow and not on top of developments. This is not a view likely to enhance career opportunities for the embassy's personnel. Of course, "timely" in Washington means Washington time. A message sent from Moscow at the end of the working day there will be on recipients' desks (or in their electronic in-boxes) at the start of the following day in Washington. This is generally a good thing—unless you send it out at the end of the workday on a Friday afternoon before, say, Memorial Day weekend, a timing gaffe almost certain to bury it. Sending messages from Tokyo or Beijing requires an entirely different timing calculus.

THE INTELLIGENCE COMMUNITY

The intelligence community, or IC as it is fondly referred to by the cognoscenti, is a many-headed animal, so wondrous strange that one would scarce believe it exists at all, but there it is. In one observer's view, the phrase "intelligence community" is an oxymoron, if by "community" one means a large organization with common goals, purposes, and direction. It, and its constituent parts, "were created and developed like most bureaucracies throughout history—haphazardly, independently, competitively, and awkwardly."[3] In the foreign affairs arena, its principal components for most of the post–World War II period have been relevant parts of the CIA, the DIA, the National Security Agency (NSA), and the INR Bureau. The reorganization following the September 11, 2001, attack on the United States has added to this mix the director of National Intelligence and elements of the Department of Homeland Security. Depending on the subject at hand, this core group may be expanded to a dozen or so agencies. For example, on nuclear matters the Department of Energy plays a key role. Each of these components is headed, ultimately, by an individual who is either a member of the president's cabinet or the functional equivalent thereof. Each brings its own particular area of expertise to the table, and each has its own bureaucratic axe to grind. Collectively, the IC's job is to bring together and assess all of the information the government possesses about a particular matter and prepare a collective judgment on it. The IC's incorrect assessment that Iraq had an active program for weapons of mass destruction[4] and its volte-face in 2007 on its assessment two years earlier that Iran had an active, clandestine nuclear weapons program have raised questions about its structure, independence, and competence that we will return to. For the purposes of this chapter, however, we want to consider it simply in its role as audience for embassy dispatches.

Much of the intelligence community is divided into operations and analytical divisions. The job of the operations division is to find things out and transmit the information to headquarters. The analytical division receives information, aggregates it, analyzes it, and provides its judgment about what it means. Analysts like information. They do not particularly care where it comes from, be it newspapers, CIA stations, NSA intercepts, or embassy dispatches. They are pretty much equal-opportunity devourers of information, although they may tend to give more credence to information that has a security classification. Analysts also like to analyze. This is, after all, their job.

As an audience, IC members will see embassy dispatches as a significant source of information, particularly valuable because the embassy officer is able to interact directly with host-country officials and other sources of information. On the other hand, they will assume, often correctly, that they have access to a greater variety of information than the person who drafted an embassy dispatch.

THE POLITICAL LEADERSHIP

Who constitutes the political leadership in U.S. foreign policy? Ultimately, of course, the president provides foreign policy direction, and it could be argued that everyone else carries it out. In reality, however, the president must delegate a degree of independent decision-making authority to others in his administration. As a first approximation, as we indicated in the prior chapter, that group includes the vice president and Senate-approved officials, with the inclusion of certain senior members of the NSC staff. At the State Department, this would include the assistant secretary level and above. Below the cabinet level, this definition of political leadership includes both political appointees and career officials. As the number of assistant and under secretaries at the State Department has expanded, along with the number of specially appointed envoys dealing with specific regions or problems, the policymaking independence of assistant secretaries has contracted. It is generally greatest on the less publically prominent functional and geographic issues. This does not mean that the assistant secretaries are not influential on major policy issues or that their views are not sought or appreciated; rather, that their ability to initiate and carry out policy on their own has waned over time.

If it can be said that all politics is local, it may not be too great a stretch to argue that all foreign policy is also domestic. Influenced on the one hand by public opinion, press coverage, critiques by the other party and outside foreign policy experts, and/or the desire for re-election, and constrained on the other by limited resources of time, energy, money, and influence, any administration conducts the country's foreign policy with one eye, and sometimes both, on the domestic impact of its decisions. For the diplomatic political analyst, one practical consequence of this is the recognition that the political leadership at the White House and the State Department does not like to be surprised, since surprise can be interpreted as lack of competence in, or control over, the nation's foreign affairs. Embassy dispatches are valued if they enable leaders to avoid being surprised, or appearing to be surprised, by developments. They may need to be reassured that something bad is not going to happen or warned that it is. They would much rather be reassured than warned, since it is difficult for anyone to look kindly upon the bearer of bad news. In the final analysis, however, they would also much rather be warned ahead of time than surprised, although they do not always foster a climate that encourages this.

We noted above that embassy views are most likely to reach the political leadership by being funneled through the country desk, perhaps in press guidance or by incorporation into the products of the intelligence community. There also exist a variety of means by which an embassy can directly influence, if not determine, who will see its dispatches.

TARGETING YOUR AUDIENCE

The following discussion is focused on what the author knows directly: the U.S. foreign affairs system. It seems fair to assume that functional equivalents exist in other diplomatic services.

1. Precedence and Distribution Indicators

During most of the post–World War II period, cables from embassies provided a rapid means of keeping the State Department informed about events abroad. The post originating the cable decided on the speed of transmission—"routine," "priority," and "immediate" were the common designators, with other possibilities such as "niact" (night action) and "flash" intended to be used only in designated circumstances. Technically, a routine cable did not cross the space between an embassy and the department any more quickly than a flash cable. But higher-precedence cables bumped lower-precedence cables out of line in the outgoing queue at post and, probably more significantly, in the incoming queue at the State Department. These queues could be significant choke points. The post also decided the security classification of the document—"unclassified," "limited official use" (now known as "SBU," for "sensitive but unclassified"), "confidential," "secret," or "top secret." The readership of the document could be further restricted by using designators such as "LIMDIS," "EXDIS," and "NODIS" ("limited," "executive," or "exclusive," and "no distribution," respectively—the last a particularly wonderful bureaucratic non sequitur) and/or a variety of code words. Code words are unique discriminators. Since each code word is itself classified, if you do not know it, you are obviously not cleared to know the contents of the code-worded document.

In theory, combined with a transmission system that was quick and efficient by the standards of the day, this provided a flexible, effective means of getting information in front of the people in Washington who needed it to make policy. Naturally, it never worked entirely as intended. The chances that someone at the policy level would see an embassy dispatch increased with the security classification and the restriction of distribution. Anyone who did not know this after completing a tour at an embassy and a tour in the department was in the wrong business. Transmitting an unclassified, routine cable containing any substantial information constituted something between a waste of time and, once again, an existential experience. You sent it off with no realistic expectation that anyone would read it. An embassy would often designate a cable secret/EXDIS in the hope that it would reach the desk of an assistant secretary. Top secret/NODIS cables often amounted to a plea for Seventh Floor attention.

Even if this system did not work exactly as intended, it worked fairly well. Periodic efforts to restore the sanctity of precedence and distribution indicators had limited and temporary effects. As the department's diplomatic presence abroad grew and the capacity of its communication system to handle incoming traffic increased exponentially, a message could no longer be expected to be passed upward simply because of its superior substantive content. Shortcuts were needed, and precedence and distribution indicators served the purpose.

2. Designating Addressees

The embassy may also specify particular offices or individuals as recipients of a cable. Such designations serve one or both of two purposes. First, they ensure that an office or individual receives a cable who might not otherwise. Second, they are another way of implicitly asking a particular office or individual to pay attention to the cable.

3. Personal Messages from the Ambassador

An ambassador may draft a message personally or choose to have a message designated as personally from him. Such messages tend to get greater attention because they invoke the ambassador's status as the president's personal representative to the country. Smart ambassadors write personal messages only when they have something they consider particularly important to say, so as not to cheapen the currency.

CASE STUDY: KENNAN'S "LONG TELEGRAM" IN THE TWENTY-FIRST CENTURY

Few would argue with the contention that the most influential embassy dispatch in modern U.S. diplomatic history was George Kennan's "Long Telegram" from Embassy Moscow in 1946, when he was deputy chief of mission. That cable, and the anonymous 1947 article in the journal *Foreign Affairs* based on it,[5] provided the intellectual framework for U.S. policy throughout the Cold War. The fact that Kennan may not always have agreed with the containment policies that subsequent U.S. administrations derived from his intellectual framework in no way detracts from the importance of his analysis.

What would have happened to Kennan's cable if it had been sent in the technological environment of, for example, July 1990, when I was political counselor in

Moscow? First of all, it would not have been the Long Telegram. It could have been Embassy Moscow cable number 23,603, there having been an average of some 3,600 cables transmitted monthly by mid-July. If we assume that the cable was classified secret and had been given an EXDIS distribution restriction, it would not have sunk without a trace. The secret designation would not have elicited much attention, but the EXDIS restriction would, paradoxically, have gotten the cable more readership, or at least more influential readership, than if there had been no restrictions on it. The Kennan cable would also have benefited from the fact that there existed a large governmental audience in Washington for political reporting from Embassy Moscow. As we indicated at the outset of this chapter, if Kennan had been reporting from, say, Embassy Reykjavík , his brilliant analysis would probably have been read only by his desk officer, a junior official responsible for two or three other countries as well.

Kennan authored his analysis, no doubt felt strongly about it, and, if he had been the ambassador, would most likely have tagged it as a personal message from him to the secretary and would have been justified in doing so. That would have ensured that it reached the secretary's office, though it could not have guaranteed that it would be put on his desk or read if it were. Kennan would certainly have gotten a reply from the secretary, though not one written by the secretary himself. Assuming again the EXDIS distribution restriction, the cable would have reached elements of the intelligence community, which might or might not have referred to it in its own products or prepared analyses either supporting or disputing Kennan's. By 2007, technology would also have allowed Kennan the opportunity for secure telephone discussions or e-mail exchanges about the content of his analysis before he transmitted it. By alerting the country desk to the analysis he was preparing to submit and requesting its help in getting the report to senior officials, he might have been able to increase the likelihood he would reach the audience he desired. Such opportunities, however, come with serious potential consequences, which we shall discuss in our final chapter.

CASE STUDY: IS KIEV RADIOACTIVE?

While political counselor at Embassy Moscow from 1988 to 1991, I periodically got middle-of-the-night phone calls from the State Department's operations center, a 24-hour-a-day, 365-day-a-year facility that monitors international developments when the rest of the bureaucracy is asleep or on vacation. These calls generally amounted to requests for reassurance. They came to me because the watch officer making the call did not want to wake up the ambassador or the deputy chief of mission. I was the third-ranking officer at the embassy, junior enough to be awakened but senior enough that the watch officer could provide a credible answer to questions from above.

I remember one of those calls vividly. Aroused from a deep sleep, I picked up the phone, and the watch officer identified himself. Groggily, I heard him say that there was a press report that Kiev was being evacuated because a nuclear accident had released radioactivity. (This was after the Chernobyl disaster.) Could I tell him anything about this? I said I'd see what I could find out and phone him back.

I sat up, put both feet on the floor, and blearily tried to figure out how in the world, sitting in Moscow at 3 a.m., I was going to be able to find out anything about a possible evacuation of Kiev. Kiev is roughly as far from Moscow as Miami is from Washington, and we had no consulate there. Moreover, unlike in the United States, this was not the sort of thing that would be on late-night TV or radio, to the extent either existed in Moscow at the time. Absolutely nothing occurred to me. I decided I had better get dressed and walk up to my office in the embassy, about a block away, hoping that sitting behind my desk there would jog my mental faculties.

About ten minutes later, sitting behind my desk, I remembered that Germany (at the time it was West Germany) had a consulate in Kiev, although I had no idea how to reach it. I phoned the German Embassy in Moscow, reached a security guard who spoke English, told him my story, convinced him that I was not a crackpot, and ascertained that his embassy had heard nothing from its Kiev consulate about a nuclear accident or an evacuation. I also got the phone number of the Kiev consulate, which I immediately phoned. I reached another security guard, who also spoke English. I was having a good night. I went through the same drill and got the same response. The guard added that he could not hear any sirens. He looked out the window and said that he could not see anyone evacuating. I phoned the operations center, which was happy to get the information and let me go back to sleep. From initial phone call to head back on pillow probably took only a little over an hour.

When I mentioned this incident at the staff meeting the next morning, everyone else was much amused. But, of course, they had slept through it.

CHAPTER FOUR

THE COMPETITION

The comic-strip philosopher Pogo famously said, "We have met the enemy and he is us." This does not satisfactorily describe the nature of your relationship with your audience, but it captures an element that the craftsman should not ignore. You exist with them in a collaborative/competitive relationship—in some cases close, in some cases distant, sometimes mostly collaborative, at other times mostly competitive. It is important to remember, however, that your audience is only a part, and not always the most important part, of your competition.

There will be those who will say, referring to diplomatic political analysis, "This is not a competition." Do not believe them. It is a competition of ideas, not necessarily zero-sum, but a competition nonetheless. It is a competition for attention, much more nearly zero-sum, since attention requires time and energy, neither in unlimited supply. It is a competition for influence, if you are doing this work because you think it matters, rather than just collecting a paycheck.

Let us look at your audience now as competitors, rather than simply as grateful recipients of the blessings of your brilliance. Then we can look at the ever-widening universe from which your other competitors can be drawn.

THE COUNTRY DESK

Ideally, and in most cases in fact, the country desk and the embassy political analyst are mutually supportive. The country desk can be of great help to the analyst, not only by encouraging a wider readership for his work, but also by letting the analyst know what issues are most on the minds of senior officials and suggesting analytical efforts that are needed or would get Washington's attention. This can help the embassy prioritize its work. It needs to be said again that time and energy are always more limited than are subjects for political analysis. Knowing what interests the leadership at home can guide, if not govern, the embassy's use of its resources. If the country desk is uniquely positioned to help the embassy understand the capital's interests and priorities, the embassy is uniquely positioned to help the country desk understand developments in the host country. As we indicated in the previous chapter, this is one of the most vital aspects of helping the desk officer achieve his own objectives. This mutual support can be the basis for a highly beneficial symbiosis.

As we briefly mentioned before, however, it is not always necessarily sweetness and light in this relationship. When the desk and the embassy interpret developments differently, the desk officer will want his view to prevail. This is perfectly natural. It would, in fact, be irresponsible of him not to seek adoption of the view he considers best corresponds to reality. This should be a competition of ideas. It can all too easily degenerate into a conflict of personalities, which serves neither the embassy analyst's interests nor those of the country he serves. Moreover, although desk officers, like embassy personnel, do not make policy, they answer to higher-ups in a chain that eventually leads to those who do and are exposed more directly to the interests and priorities of the policymakers. Personal contact is the best way to keep the competitive side of this relationship from becoming antagonistic. The embassy reporting officer should visit the country desk before departing on assignment abroad and whenever back in the capital. He should seek out the person or persons on the desk who will be most interested in the issues on which he will be reporting and get their ideas. This will be helpful as he orients himself initially at post. It will also enable him, as he is brought into his job at the embassy, to mentally highlight issues where there may be some divergence of view between the embassy and the desk. Finally, when he sends in something that the desk officer disagrees with, it will help the latter remember that there is a person and a professional at the other end of the line, not an irresponsible flake.

THE INTELLIGENCE COMMUNITY

Washington analysts, naturally, want to do their own analysis, rather than be the passive recipients of embassy analyses. While it is fair to say that they value embassy input, it is also true that some, although unlikely to say so for the record, would prefer embassies to confine their dispatches to reporting—that is, to providing information about *what* is happening. What the happenings mean—the *why*, the heart of analysis—they prefer to interpret for themselves. (This parallels the separation of much of the intelligence community into operations and analytical divisions.) Of course, no embassy political or economic officer worth his salt would ever agree to such a division of labor, but this tension may nevertheless exist. Moreover, the various elements of the Washington intelligence community have established vehicles—the President's Daily Brief, the National Intelligence Estimate, etc.—for getting their views before policymakers. Only in exceptional circumstances, such as in a personal message from the ambassador to the secretary of state, do such vehicles exist for embassy reporting. Embassy analytical efforts, if noted at all in intelligence community products, most likely reach policymakers incorporated as one among a number of elements in an existing intelligence vehicle. The embassy has no control over how, or whether, its reporting and analytical work is going to be reflected in intelligence analyses.

At least some members of the intelligence community—generally the higher-ranking ones—will periodically be able to visit the country. They may have, or develop, contacts of their own. The visits and the contacts are valuable for obvious reasons. Even a short visit can freshen the insights of knowledgeable analysts. There may also, however, be some bureaucratic gamesmanship involved in this. Back home, the intelligence analyst, armed with the insights of a recent trip, will be more likely to insist upon the accuracy of his own view. Like other visitors, he may have a tendency to overestimate the importance of what he has personally observed and heard, as well as the access and accuracy of his personal contacts.

VISITING FIREMEN

Embassies receive a constant stream of visitors: many official, some unofficial but nevertheless influential. Indeed, from the embassy's perspective, this stream often seems an ever-widening and -deepening torrent, and managing it may come to be seen, particularly by the visitors, as the embassy's chief raison d'être. Many of these visitors are there to see and learn about the country firsthand, perhaps even to develop some personal contacts locally. This is a good thing. Some years ago, the press learned that an NSC staffer, hired for his expertise on Soviet affairs, had never visited the Soviet Union. Asked about it, the staffer said that he had never been hit by a truck either but knew he wouldn't like it. Eventually, he did visit. I do not personally know whether he learned anything but would like to believe so.

The amount of time and energy that goes into the care and feeding of "visiting firemen" varies greatly from embassy to embassy. In all cases, it is time and energy that is taken away from traditional embassy political work but often offers otherwise un-available opportunities for influence. In the weeks prior to a visit by the president or the secretary of state, an embassy effectively does nothing other than prepare for the visit. It is hard to argue that this is not how it should be. Aside from the country desk officer and the intelligence community, visitors may come from other parts of the State Department, from other civilian agencies of the government, from the military, from other branches of the government, from the business community, or from a variety of interest groups. Each will return home touting his new or updated expertise. Many will ask for, or be offered, embassy briefings, which they may or may not pay close attention to. A few will consider that they should be briefing the embassy, rather than the reverse.

The face-to-face contact afforded by these visits carries with it both opportunity and risk. In addition to the previously mentioned opportunity to influence the visitor's outlook, embassy personnel may be able to raise their own visibility. The risks are that the visitor will go away unimpressed, more inclined to reject the embassy's views and to discount the value of his interlocutors at the embassy. All such visits give embassy officers the opportunity to hone their oral briefing skills. Visitors may expect and receive high-quality written briefing materials, but they do not always give them much attention. The embassy officer needs to view these written analyses as the admission ticket to his own performance. In a sense, this is the price he has to pay in order to persuade the audience that he has the right credentials. The performance is his personal interaction with the visitor, sometimes in the guise of a formal oral briefing, more often informally.

I met with a lot of visitors in Moscow. I would have to assess my own record in dealing with them as spotty at best. I recall a couple of these interactions. In spring 1991, I briefed at his request the vice president of an important American firm that was looking into opportunities in what was then the Soviet Union. At an early stage of the conversation, he asked how solid I thought Soviet president Gorbachev's position was. I replied that I thought his chances of completing his term in office were less than fifty-fifty. Although I went on to explain my reasoning, I later realized that I had lost credibility with him as soon as I gave those odds. They were too far outside of his frame of reference for understanding how the Soviet system worked. In retrospect, I recognized that I should have led him through my reasoning before dropping the bottom line on him.

When Iraq invaded Kuwait on August 2, 1990, Secretary of State James Baker was visiting Mongolia. He flew to Moscow a day later for a meeting with Soviet foreign minister Eduard Shevardnadze, primarily to discuss the invasion. I accompanied two of his senior advisers on the ride in from Sheremetyevo airport to the embassy. Their location at the time of the invasion and their travels since had kept them pretty out of touch with developments on this issue. I was troubled, however, that as the two of them discussed it, they seemed to consider it a relatively minor event, and they were not discussing the aspect of it that I considered most significant. I did not think that Secretary Baker should carry this assessment of the situation into his meeting with Shevardnadze. During a pause in their conversation with one another, I remarked that preventing Saddam Hussein from controlling Kuwait's oilfields struck me as a fairly vital U.S. interest. I did not say anything more on the subject, since I knew that one of the advisers was a rather prickly, egotistical character, more likely to take offense at my presumption in offering my view of U.S. interests than to appreciate the input. Happily, by the time Baker met with Shevardnadze, he was fully briefed on the issue and began the discussions that produced a remarkable level of cooperation between the two countries in the months preceding the armed liberation of Kuwait. Let me be clear that I have no reason to believe that my remark to his advisers had anything to do with Baker getting up to speed on this issue. It is more likely that he was on the right track by the time he met with Shevardnadze because he had been brought up to date by Washington. The point is that, in dealing with visiting firemen, the embassy political analyst's job is to say the right thing at the right time to the people with whom he is dealing. In this case, I felt that I had done my job. Lots of times, that is all there is. If you do not find that satisfying, if you prefer more glamour or recognition, you may be in the wrong business.

CONGRESSIONAL AND CONGRESSIONAL STAFF DELEGATIONS

I do not know how it is with other diplomatic services, but the U.S. Foreign Service is rife with stories about the nightmares occasioned by visits of members of the legislative branch. Most of these stories contain more of diplomatic folklore than of accuracy and generally involve alcohol and/or persons of the opposite sex. I have nothing to add to this folklore, since I never witnessed any inappropriate behavior involving either. Problematic visitors are not a monopoly of the legislative branch. Of the two most inappropriate visitors I had the misfortune to be involved with, one was on the staff of a congressional committee, the other was a political appointee assistant secretary with the State Department. The staffer's behavior was the more egregious. I had arranged a meeting for him with the foreign minister of a francophone African state. After posing a tendentious question to the foreign minister and not getting the answer he was looking for, the staffer turned to me and said, "Let's get out of here. This is a waste of my time." The foreign minister, who had been speaking in French, understood English, something the staffer either had not considered or did not care about. Our ambassador later apologized to the foreign minister on behalf of the U.S. government. The staffer went on to embarrass other embassies. The assistant secretary in question brought his wife and infant child with him on his visit. In order for his wife to attend official meetings with him, he had embassy political officers babysit the child and do the family laundry.

There is a certain heightened level of tension in congressional visits that is normally not found in executive branch visits unless they involve the president or secretary of state. Possibly, this is a reflection on the local level of the American system of checks and balances between the three branches of government. For whatever reason, congressional delegations tend to be sensitive about their prerogatives and quick to perceive slights, whether real or imagined. For the embassy political officer, the opportunities and risks are the same as with other delegations, except that the stakes may be higher and the margins for error lower in dealing with congressional visitors than with most other visitors. This is particularly true if the congressional visitors are from the Senate Foreign Relations Committee, which can effectively kill an ambassadorial nomination, or with the Senate or House Appropriations Committee because of their role in the budgetary process. A member of Congress or, for that matter, a key staffer who takes a personal interest in issues involving the country where you serve, can play a very significant role in U.S. policy toward that country, particularly in providing or denying funds. If you have seen the film *Charlie Wilson's War,* you get the idea, although perhaps in exaggerated form.

THE MEDIA

The important thing for the embassy political analyst about media coverage is its political impact in the home country. For political leaders at home, mass perception is political reality. It has to be dealt with. It is a priority—sometimes *the* priority. The media may not only usurp the attention of the political leadership, they may also determine what issues it considers important.

CNN has revolutionized international reporting. There is no way that embassy reporting of events can match the drama and immediacy of a live feed from a television network. Former Deputy Secretary of State Strobe Talbott illustrated this vividly in his description of being in the midst of an unclassified telephone conversation with a Russian deputy foreign minister while both were watching CNN's televised, real-time coverage of Russian troops storming the legislature in 1993.[1] During my time in Moscow, a period of dramatic change in the Soviet Union, major American newspapers provided virtually unlimited space to their Moscow correspondents, many of whom responded with admirable work. Even an experienced, energetic, and prolific embassy political section had difficulty matching the output of Moscow's corps of foreign journalists, nor, it became increasingly clear, should it have tried. Rather, its factual reporting needed to focus on significant events that for one reason or another did not reach the attention of the foreign press corps. And its analytical efforts, at least in part, needed to provide a context for the flood of press and TV coverage coming out of Moscow. One of the best political analysts the State Department has produced says that "embassy reporting must add value to what policymakers learn from news reports; it cannot hope to substitute for or compete with news organs in reporting 'fast facts'. . . . The value of an embassy report is to tell policymakers what they need to know and to sort out what's important from all the other things Washington is hearing."[2]

This was particularly true when I served in Moscow because, collectively, foreign press reporting out of Moscow sometimes created impressions in the West that were quite wide of Soviet reality. For example, in late 1990, American and European readers of press headlines could easily have believed that famine and a spontaneous mass migration of Soviet citizens to the West were imminent.[3] The overall grain harvest that year was the largest in Soviet history, a fact that the embassy had reported. Mass starvation was not going to occur in a year of record grain harvests, even when rampant waste and growing distribution difficulties were factored in.[4] (Ironically, the Western press was much slower on the uptake in subsequent years, when declining grain harvests and even greater distribution breakdowns made widespread hunger a real threat.) Moreover, even if there had been widespread hunger, geographic distances precluded a mass march on Western Europe, and there were not enough trains, planes, and automobiles to transport hundreds of thousands to the borders, let alone millions. Ultimately, the embassy made these points in a cable advising Washington that distribution problems might produce some localized food shortages but not famine.[5] This met the department's pressing need, which was to provide something reassuring to policymakers and, more specifically, to the State and White House officials taking questions from the press at their daily briefings. Western European leaders rushed to provide food aid to help Soviet president Gorbachev meet a nonexistent humanitarian crisis at a time when he was resisting adoption of a comprehensive reform plan. U.S. leaders understood that this was a political, not a humanitarian, issue and, while ultimately agreeing to provide loans for food purchases, appeared to share the embassy's view that assistance could be counterproductive if it enabled the Soviet leadership to delay or avoid adopting a comprehensive economic reform program.

The embassy analyst must resist the temptation to dismiss media coverage that he considers inaccurate or focused on the unimportant, because his audience at home will not dismiss it. As we have discussed previously, this competition provides once again both an opportunity and a risk. If the leadership at home is focused on an issue because of media coverage, a timely embassy analysis can reach and influence that leadership. In this context, a late report is often the functional equivalent of no report. The opportunity to influence has been lost, and the question of embassy competence has been raised. The press/embassy reporting competition can appear unequal at times. As one recipient of the Director General's Award for Reporting (to be discussed further in chapter 7) puts it:

> It was very discouraging when the press corps had more credibility than I did. There were multiple occasions when I would report over a period of time on something, not to hear back from Washington until it showed up in a *New York Times* or *Washington Post* story. At that point, I'd get a call or cable asking why I hadn't reported on the topic and instructing me to learn about it right away.[6]

Washington has a a short attention span and a short memory. As Ambassador Jack Matlock, who had previously been the NSC's director for European affairs, used to say to his staff in Moscow, "If you haven't told it to Washington within the past three months, you never told it to Washington." This is not likely to change.

ACADEMIA AND THE THINK TANKS

There was a time in the early days of the American republic when the secretary of state was a significant figure in his own right and a likely future president. Clearly, that is generally no longer the case in the United States, although the present secretary, Hillary Clinton, does have significant political standing of her own. In most countries, the foreign minister is not a person of independent political significance, but rather an adviser to the country's leader who brings to the job certain generally accepted credentials in the foreign policy field. In the United States, this has created a revolving door between universities and think tanks, such as the Carnegie Endowment and the Hoover Institution on the one hand, and the State Department and the NSC on the other. Academia and the think tanks are sometimes parking places for foreign affairs specialists associated with the party out of power or who are themselves temporarily out of favor with the current foreign policy leadership. Successful academics who attach themselves to political campaigns as policy advisers may wind up at very high foreign-policy levels, as secretaries of state Henry Kissinger, Zbigniew Brzezinski, Madeleine Albright, and Condoleeza Rice can attest.

There are two kinds of academic foreign affairs specialists: those who approach the field primarily from a research perspective and those who approach it primarily from a policy perspective. There is very little overlap between these groups. They barely speak the same language and rarely read the same publications. The researcher will publish in journals such as the *American Political Science Review* and the *Journal of Conflict Resolution*. You will find the "policy wonk" in *Foreign Affairs*, *Foreign Policy*, various regional journals, and on the op-ed page of major newspapers.

I can still remember the pride with which one of my graduate school professors, whose approach to foreign affairs emphasized quantitative analysis, announced one day that his latest research had accounted for all of the variance in international conflict. This was the functional equivalent of Francis Fukuyama announcing the end of history, although it attracted a good deal less attention, probably because my professor's research was incomprehensible to all but a few academic acolytes of his methodological approach. In any case, international conflict, like history, went on, even with all its variance explained, and so did I, to take part in foreign affairs rather than research it.

Think tank and academic foreign policy and geographic region specialists provide much of the intellectual underpinning for policymaking within government. They occupy a kind of intellectual sweet spot between the evanescence of daily journalism and the operationalism of much of the governmental foreign policy apparatus. They usually come to identify themselves, and to be identified, with a major political party. If their party is in power, their first choice is to be in policymaking positions within the government; their second choice is to be on the outside, generally supportive, but drafting pieces that subtly suggest that things would be even better if their hand were at the helm. If their party is not in power, of course, they are not likely to approve of the policies then being implemented.

The diplomatic analyst who stays abreast of these intellectual trends has a better chance of shaping his own analysis in ways that improve its chances of getting a readership at home. This does not mean altering the facts, interpretations, or conclusions to fit a particular outlook. Rather, it means using a terminology that is current in the capital and addressing issues that are important in the foreign policy discourse. At times, a particular journal article or book may become required reading within the governmental foreign policy apparatus, probably because someone at a high level in the administration has mentioned it favorably, and everyone wants to be seen as commenting knowingly on it. There is a lot of gamesmanship in this, but it is gamesmanship that the analyst abroad may not want to ignore. If he is properly connected with the country desk at home, he can be kept informed when these intellectual mini-trends develop. This allows him to make an informed decision about whether or not to reflect them in his analyses, which is certainly better than simply proceeding in ignorance of them.

This chapter and the one preceding it have been concerned with the analyst's audience and competition, with a view toward ensuring the usefulness of his analysis. Work that is not timely, that does not engage its intended audience, or is not cognizant of its competition will not be useful. I like to think of usefulness as a necessary but not sufficient condition for effective political analysis. Political analysis may be good without being useful, but it cannot be useful if it is not also good. We turn our attention in the next two chapters to a set of tools that I believe can contribute to higher quality work.

CHAPTER FIVE

THE ANALYST'S PERSONAL TOOLKIT

A disclaimer is in order. There are hundreds and hundreds of books available about political analysis. This chapter does not survey or summarize them. Rather, it offers my views about the knowledge and conceptual tools that I found useful during a career devoted primarily to doing diplomatic political analysis. Like the rest of this book, it is a personal perspective rather than an academic study. The reader should take what he can use and leave the rest.

I find it useful to think of these analytical tools as falling into three categories:

- Personal tools
- Analytical tools that can be used everywhere
- Analytical tools that are specific to a country

Personal tools are those that the analyst controls. They include linguistic and cultural competence, writing style, and sources and contacts. In principle, the breadth and depth of the analyst's abilities in each of these areas is limited only by his own talent and energy. These tools are the subject matter of this chapter. The others will be covered in the next chapter.

CULTURAL UNDERSTANDING

The ideal diplomatic political dispatch would be complete, accurate, correctly predictive, and timely. The good diplomatic political dispatch recognizes that compromises must be made among these qualities and finds the right balance for the subject matter and circumstances at hand. Chapter 2 describes a hypothetical conflict between the demands of completeness and timeliness. In the real world, the political officer faces that particular conflict on a daily basis.

If completeness involves having all the facts, accuracy obviously involves getting the facts right. At first blush, facts would seem to be hard, tangible things. Something either is, or it is not. Facts provide the basis of analysis and support for opinion. Separating the two is essential but not always straightforward. How often have we heard that one person's fact is another person's opinion? Reporting what someone has told you is factual reporting. In the chapter 2 example, it is a fact that the head of the mineworkers' union told the political officer that his union would go on strike at noon the next day. That did not necessarily mean that the union would actually do so. Suppose the union chief rolled his eyes and squirmed in his chair while he said this. Those are also facts, but are they relevant to what he said? Do they indicate that he may be lying, that he is under pressure, or that he has a stomach ailment? Does he think that his office is bugged and he is actually delivering a message to the authorities, while ostensibly providing information to you? Facts sometimes speak for themselves. Often, they require context in order to be meaningful. In supplying context, the political officer moves from reporting to analysis and prediction. He brings to bear more of the tools of his trade, including his linguistic and cultural competence.

Diplomacy thrives on linguistic competence and cultural immersion. The ideal diplomat would speak the host country's language like a native, be so immersed in the local culture as to be able to think like a native, and would never forget that he is not one—that he is there to represent his own country's interests. I have known one or two diplomats who come close to that ideal, although I do not count myself among them.[1]

Much of diplomatic political analysis involves filtering out the noise so as to isolate the information—in other words, distinguishing the significant from the trivial. In most contemporary societies, diplomats are awash in what passes for information but which, for their purposes, is usually noise. The diplomat's job is to hear what is significant in that cacophony of voices. In closed societies, particularly totalitarian ones, information in the traditional sense is in short supply. Information is, or can be, power in all societies, but in totalitarian ones it is also a weapon and is treated as such. In closed societies, one often learns as much from what is *not* said as from what is said.

Linguistic competence and cultural understanding are two of the most important tools the diplomat uses to filter, prioritize, and interpret information. During the Cold War, use of these tools to analyze developments in the Soviet Union came to be known as Kremlinology. Both diplomats and journalists practiced Kremlinology, although not always to universal approval. In the summer and fall of 1963, a young political officer in Moscow named Jack Matlock drafted several cables reporting that opposition to Communist Party general secretary Nikita Khrushchev was developing and that there was evidence that it was led by Politburo member Leonid Brezhnev. The political counselor and the ambassador cleared the cables, and the embassy transmitted them to Washington. Although these cables were both good and timely, they were not what an important part of the Washington audience wanted to hear. Matlock recalls that former ambassador to Moscow Llewellyn Thompson, then a senior Soviet adviser at the State Department, was furious. Much of Thompson's reputation in Washington rested on his relationship with Khrushchev, and he did not like to see reports that Khrushchev's power might be threatened. He sent the director of the Soviet desk to the embassy with the message that it should "knock off the silly Kremlinology." Happily, the embassy at the time had a political counselor, Richard E. Davies, with some of the attributes that distinguish a bull from a steer. He replied that "so long as the Department pays my admittedly pitiful retainer and the ambassador approves the messages, we report things as we see them!"[2] He and Matlock went on to highly distinguished diplomatic careers following Thompson's departure from the State Department, something political officers tempted toward self-censorship for fear of annoying important people might keep in mind. There are no guarantees, but sometimes people do remember when you get it right.

In the early 1980s, a Moscow-based journalist who spoke Russian and knew the Soviet Union scooped the world by reporting the night before it was officially announced that Soviet leader Konstantin Chernenko had probably died. The reporter had been up late that night listening to the radio, when the program suddenly switched to somber classical music. He checked, and all other stations that were on the air had done the same. He knew that this had become standard practice when a leader died and also knew that Chernenko had not been in good health. His newspaper buried the story on an inside page after checking with a State Department official who should have known better but instead asked the editor who inquired about the report whether the journalist was smoking something he should not be. That State Department official went on to a very distinguished diplomatic career, which demonstrates that sometimes people do not remember when you get it wrong.

It may seem almost a truism that cultural sensitivity is needed when dealing with other countries. Truism or not, the reality is that even experienced diplomats often fail to apply their theoretical understanding of a country's culture to how they carry out their actual activities. The gaffes made by linguistically and culturally challenged visiting firemen range from the humorous to the painful to the potentially dangerous. On one occasion during a meeting at the Foreign Ministry in Moscow, I listened in embarrassment as the adviser to a high-ranking State Department official explained "the Russian soul" for about forty-five minutes to the primarily Russian officials present. He knew no Russian, had never lived in the country, and had not studied it professionally. This would have been totally inappropriate even if he had, but of course if he had he would presumably have known better. Afterward, he asked me how I thought it had gone. He seemed nonplussed when I replied, possibly more frankly than I should have, that, as a general rule, I found it more useful to have Russians tell me about the Russian soul than for me to tell them about it. Dealing with visitors on matters of this kind is a delicate matter. You do not want to reinforce culturally insensitive behavior, but neither do you want to alienate your visitors, since it is in your interest to have them conveying good impressions of the embassy and of you personally to people back home. The politically and bureaucratically smart reply would have been more anodyne. My personal toolkit was at times a bit light in this area.

During my first tour in Moscow in the late 1970s, the embassy hosted a thirteen-member delegation of U.S. senators, whose schedule called for them to visit Leningrad and then Minsk before coming on to Moscow. This was an unusually large delegation of senators and an important one, since the Senate would soon be deciding whether to approve an arms control treaty. The Soviet leadership was fully cognizant of the delegation's significance and pulled out all the stops to ensure a successful visit, including arranging meetings with the top Communist Party leaders in Leningrad and Minsk, both of whom were Politburo members. I met up with the delegation in Minsk, where I had been tasked to head the embassy's advance team. Some of the senators were unhappy. They did not think their delegation was being taken seriously—they felt they were not meeting with sufficiently senior people. I was still young and inexperienced enough to be flabbergasted. Here were U.S. senators who would have been the first to say that this was a totalitarian society but did not understand that the centralized leadership in such a society would be located in the capital, which they had not yet gotten to. Here were U.S. senators who knew that this was a communist country but did not understand that in meeting with the highest-ranking Communist Party official in each city they visited, they were meeting with the country's top leaders, each of whom was incomparably more powerful than any U.S. official, except perhaps the president.

My boss, who had accompanied the delegation from Leningrad, was more savvy and took this as an opportunity to convey some information about how the Soviet Union worked. He happened also to understand the U.S. political culture pretty well and managed to do this without bruising any senatorial egos, a good example, in my view, of how a smart political officer can use an oral briefing both to educate his audience and correct misimpressions that might otherwise cause influential visitors to depart with an unnecessarily jaundiced memory of their visit.

LINGUISTIC COMPETENCE

Linguistic competence presumably does not require much definition. It concerns how well you speak, read, write, and understand a foreign language. Higher levels of ability allow the practitioner to pick up oral or written cues that may completely elude the less competent. While more language competence is always better than less, it is also important to avoid the hubris of overestimating one's competence. In a social setting, using the host country's language has the dual virtues of politeness and enabling one's abilities to improve. In a negotiation, the diplomat with less than native speaking ability disadvantages himself on several counts. He cannot express his country's position as clearly and cogently as he should. He risks missing something important in what the other side says or in how it is said. He risks becoming more focused on the linguistic challenges of the process than on the substantive ones. A diplomat should never hesitate to use an interpreter. In fact, using interpretation in formal negotiations may be preferable, even for the linguistically adept. Pauses for interpretation allow the negotiations to proceed at a more measured pace. Tactically speaking, the more linguistically adept side in a negotiation is the side more advantaged by using an interpreter. The diplomat who has understood the other side's remarks can begin to formulate his own response while listening with one ear for any nuances he may have missed. The diplomat who has not understood the other side's remarks must spend the time entirely focused on listening to the interpretation. Furthermore, the linguistically competent diplomat can listen to the interpreter's translation of his own remarks to ensure that they are correctly expressed. Even highly skilled interpreters can make slips in areas outside their expertise. They want to get it right, and, while it is not good form to correct trivialities, they will appreciate the opportunity to clarify any significant misstatement. Finally, listening to the other side's questions and comments made to the interpreter can yield information about their sensitivities or areas of potential flexibility.

UNDERSTANDING CULTURAL DIFFERENCES

Cultural competence may be more subject to misinterpretation. It should be clear that the term is used here in a very broad sense. It encompasses understanding who has power, authority, and influence in the country and what they are doing with it. It involves understanding the underlying forces at work in a society that affect the political arena. The list of such forces is potentially endless. Among them are demography, social structure, income distribution, economy, education, nationalism, history, religion, and ethnicity. No single diplomatic political analysis can cover all of these forces, nor should it. The diplomat's job is to determine which of them are significant at a given point in time or in a given situation and to assess their effects. How and in what circumstances, for example, would one want to consider the impact of the "baby boomer" generation in the United States? The percentage of the population aged under twenty in certain developing countries? The precipitous population decline in Russia?

It is possible to understand a foreign culture without being fully cognizant of the implications of cultural differences. Cultural differences produce widely varying negotiating styles, which can affect anything ranging from getting a seat at a restaurant to concluding an arms control treaty. Even experienced diplomats are often less attuned to cultural differences in negotiating style in the absence of visual cues to those differences. Let me put this more plainly. Although the U.S. diplomatic service is happily moving toward a diversity that reflects our society as a whole, it is predominantly white and middle class. I believe that U.S. diplomats generally expect that there will be cultural differences when dealing with Asians or Africans, particularly if they are dressed in their society's business attire, rather than in Western style. We are less likely to expect such differences when dealing with, for example, Russians, who look just like the average middle-class white European or American. We are more likely to make allowance for those differences with Asians and Africans, and more likely to get angry when Russians do not behave the way we expect them to. The reality is that Russians come from a culture that did not experience the Renaissance, the Reformation, or the Enlightenment; that they experience authority relationships totally differently from the way Americans do; and that they come from a high-context culture (one that interprets meaning primarily from context rather than from the words spoken), while we come from a low-context culture (one that tends to focus on the words rather than the context). Recognizing these cultural differences is not simply an intellectual exercise. It is essential to interpreting the behavior of those on the other side of the negotiating table.[3]

STYLE

There are diplomats brilliantly talented in foreign languages and well connected in the host country who cannot write a coherent sentence in their own native language. Their dispatches fail to achieve the two essential objectives of any diplomatic political analysis. The analysis must: (a) present its information and interpretation clearly and (b) present it in a way that makes the audience want to read it. There is no magic stylistic formula for achieving this objective, but there are many ways of failing to achieve it. Below are the opening sentences from two of the most renowned historical/political analyses of all time:

Gaul is divided into three parts, one of which the Belgae inhabit, another the Aquitani, the third those who in their own language are called Celts, in ours Gauls. They differ from each other in language, customs and laws. The river Garonne separates the Gauls from the Aquitani; the Marne and the Seine separate them from the Belgae. The Belgae are the bravest among them, because they are farthest from the civilization and refinement of [our] Province, and merchants least frequently visit and sell them those things which tend to effeminate the mind; further, they are the nearest to the Germans, who dwell beyond the Rhine, with whom they are continually waging war.[4]

In the second century of the Christian era, the empire of Rome comprehended the fairest part of the earth, and the most civilized portion of mankind. The frontiers of that extensive monarchy were guarded by ancient renown and disciplined valor. The gentle but powerful influence of laws and manners had gradually cemented the union of the provinces. Their peaceful inhabitants enjoyed and abused the advantages of wealth and luxury. The image of a free constitution was preserved with decent reverence: the Roman senate appeared to possess the sovereign authority, and devolved on the emperors all the executive powers of government.[5]

Both excerpts provide a great deal of information and interpretation in very few words. Stylistically, however, they could hardly be more different. The passage from Caesar, whose contemporaries considered him a superb draftsman, suffers inevitably from having been translated from his native Latin. Having read the original as a second-year student of Latin in high school, I confess that I did not see it then as I see it now. Then, it was painful and difficult, but that owed more to my age and inability than to the subject matter. Now, I see a style that any analyst would do well to emulate:

simple, direct, concise. The second passage, from Gibbon, is another matter. His felicity as a stylist of the English language is matched only by his mastery of the subject matter. His images soar; his metaphors beguile. I have traveled some fourteen hundred years of Western civilization with Gibbon, marveling at his erudition and delighted by his language. Yet, how many times have I had to read a passage a second and a third time to grasp its meaning? No more, perhaps, than this great work deserves but many more than the diplomat's audience will. Gibbon himself may have recognized the short attention span of those on high when, as he presented the second volume of his work to the Duke of Gloucester, that worthy reportedly remarked to him, "Another damned thick, square book! Always scribble, scribble, scribble! Eh! Mr. Gibbon?"[6]

The diplomatic craftsman has no more than one chance to grab his audience's attention and convey his meaning. Form should not triumph over content. Writing style should be the unobtrusive servant of meaning, not its master. It is perfectly legitimate for the craftsman to alter his style deliberately to match it more gracefully to his subject matter, but whenever he is tempted by a rhetorical flourish he would do well to remember Caesar's *Gallic Wars*.

As a practical matter, he should also have a compelling subject line and brief summary paragraph, particularly if he hopes that his work will catch the attention of the staff people who filter hundreds of reports a day to select the few that they will place in the "read" folders of their assistant or under secretaries.

CONTACTS AND SOURCES

For our purposes, let us consider as a source anyone or anything from whom or which you get information that you use in your work. In this sense, a source can be, among other things, a person, a document, or something you observe. A contact is a person with whom you have become acquainted in the host country. It can be a government official, a diplomat from another embassy, or someone totally unconnected with governmental or political affairs. A contact may primarily be a source, occasionally a source, or never a source. In some senses, this is little different from business and personal relationships in nondiplomatic life.

A closed, authoritarian society can limit your access to sources and contacts, and produce relationships that are complex and ambiguous. During my first assignment in the Soviet Union, Soviet citizens knew that repeated contact with foreigners would bring the KGB to their door. Earlier, during parts of Stalin's rule, arrest and imprisonment or internal exile might have been the result. Later, they recognized that an accidental, one-time meeting would not threaten them. Starved for information about the rest of the world, when such opportunities arose they often seized them avidly, peppering the foreigner with questions that would enable them in one way or another to compare life in the Soviet Union with life elsewhere. Rarely, however, would they agree to a second meeting. The exceptions were generally persons on the margins of Soviet society—artists and musicians whose artistic bent did not meet official approval anyway, members of minority groups seeking permission to emigrate, and a few courageous human rights activists.

It may be useful to distinguish between required sources and interesting contacts. Required sources are those you need in order to carry out your job at the embassy. For example, if you are responsible for following country X's foreign policy in the Middle East, you will need to get to know the people in the Foreign Ministry responsible for country X's policy toward the Middle East. You will want to get to know some of the key nongovernmental Middle Eastern specialists in academia or the media. You will need to read domestic press, magazine, and journal articles on the subject. In addition to required sources, do not forget that nothing in your job description precludes you from also developing relationships with local people who share some of your personal interests.

During my two tours in Moscow, I became interested in Russian jazz and became acquainted with a Muscovite who, although not himself a musician, was a jazz aficionado and intensely involved in the local jazz scene. Through him, I became acquainted with some of the country's best jazz musicians, found out where and when local concerts were being held, and got tickets that might otherwise have been unavailable to me. Over time, through this shared interest, a friendship developed between us. Occasionally, I wrote an embassy dispatch about jazz in the Soviet Union, primarily from the point of view of how this form of music, with its frankly American roots, officially ignored although no longer actively suppressed, found outlets in the society. When I did so, he sometimes became a source, although he did not know it. As an American diplomat, I could not assume that he was not an active member of the Soviet intelligence services, although I doubted it. I did assume that he was approached from time to time by those services and asked about me. I never forgot this during our interactions, but I also did not hold it against him. This was the price he had to pay for maintaining relationships with embassy personnel who shared his musical interests.

Relationships such as these, pleasant in their own right, also help enhance one's ability to understand the social and cultural dynamics of the host country. They help establish the cultural understanding needed for good analysis.

CHAPTER SIX

THE ANALYTICAL TOOLS

Certain analytical tools can be used only in specific countries. Many of these are obvious—for example, knowledge of the country's laws and governmental structures—and I do not discuss them here. Two tools warrant additional attention: (1) political culture and (2) personalities and charisma.

Much of this chapter deals with underlying political forces that operate in any society. Understanding them provides a framework that the analytical craftsman can use as he approaches each new job. The political forces I have found important are ideology, the process of social change, the intensity and violence of conflict, rigidity or flexibility of the political structure, and probability analysis versus risk management. We deal first with these general concepts and then with those that are country specific.

ANALYTICAL TOOLS OF GENERAL APPLICABILITY
Ideological Conviction and the Right to Rule

One of the perennial debates among students of international affairs concerns the relative roles of ideology and realpolitik in determining a country's behavior in the international arena. Westerners often think of ideology in terms of a visionary or fanatical belief system. It is traditionally defined more broadly and more correctly as the body of ideas reflecting the social needs and aspirations of an individual, group, class, or culture, or as a set of doctrines or beliefs that form the basis of a political, economic, or other system.[1] An ideology does not have to be extreme to lead to extremism. The core values of Enlightenment ideology were reason and tolerance. The ideas of the Enlightenment led to the American and French revolutions, with very different short-term outcomes.

Rational outside observers, a group which presumably includes the preponderance of diplomats, tend to distrust ideology, particularly in its more extreme forms. They may even doubt that it exists, except perhaps as a tool used with deliberation by the ruling class to maintain power and manipulate the populace. This may sometimes be true. More often, it is not. The operative ideology of the ruling class may not be the same as the one it conveys to the masses, but it almost certainly has one. A ruling class is sustained by an ideology, by a core set of beliefs that convince its members that what they are doing for their own good is also for the good of their society. A stable society contains a ruling class that rests on a strong ideological base. If one considers stability a virtue, one should wish for a society with a widely accepted ideology that legitimizes the class in power.

This is not the case in much of the Third World, which is governed by ruling cliques, devoid of any ideological base or commitment. This leads to a dreary succession of coups, with each new leader and his cronies motivated by little more than a desire to get rich as quickly as they can, stay in power for as long as they can, and get out alive when they have to. Third World regimes with staying power, whether Muammar el-Qadaffi's in Libya, Ruhollah Khomeini's in Iran, or Fidel Castro's in Cuba, are likely to either import or create an ideology that justifies their right to rule to both themselves and the populace.

It would be difficult to find an example of a ruling class that did not wish to remain in power, but that wish must be distinguished clearly from a belief in its right to rule. A ruling class bereft of a belief in its right to rule will not long endure, no matter how overwhelming its power appears to be. Consider the trajectory of ideology in the former Soviet Union. Lenin created a convincing ideological structure, well adapted to the Russian political culture. The first generation of Soviet leaders, affirmed by the success of the 1917 revolution, internalized this ideology and conveyed it successfully to enough of the populace to defeat the ancien régime's counterrevolution. Stalin's purges of the ruling class during the 1930s superimposed a culture of fear on the ruling Marxist-Leninist ideology. World War II grafted elements of an old ideology, defense of the Motherland, onto this mix and brought a young, new generation into the ruling class, a group that had risen rapidly during the late 1930s as their elders were purged and that now led the country to victory in what their countrymen knew as the Great Patriotic War. That generation took control in 1964 with the ouster of Nikita Khrushchev and maintained control for the next twenty years, sustained by its members' belief that they had validated the rightness of their worldview and obtained their right to rule by saving the country from Nazi conquest. By the early 1980s, as the octogenarian members of that generation passed away one by one, there no longer existed in the Soviet Union an ideology capable of sustaining the next ruling-class generation, which had not participated in the Great Patriotic War and which, while still attached to key elements of Marxist-Leninist thinking, knew that there was no content to the formal trappings of it that still festooned the country's political life.[2] The new ruling elite, led by Mikhail Gorbachev, began a reform process intended initially to restore what it saw as the true values of Marxism-Leninism and to justify continued rule by a reformed and reinvigorated Communist Party. Gorbachev struggled throughout his rule to reconcile his essentially reformist mindset with, on the one hand, the status quo outlook of most party apparatchiks and, on the other, the increasingly revolutionary process that he had put into motion. A small group of reactionary political figures—motivated, it appears, by little more than nostalgia for the Soviet Union's real or imagined past glory and lacking any conviction in what they were doing—attempted a coup in 1991 intended to reverse reforms then under way. Instead, they precipitated what they feared and sought to prevent: the dissolution of the Soviet Union and the final discrediting of their country's putative ideology.

The spectrum of ideological adherence in any society can range from utter conviction to total disbelief. The ruling class and the populace may be at the same or at widely differing locations on this spectrum. They may not even be on the same spectrum, with the ruling class holding to one set of values and the ruled to another, a situation rife with the potential for instability, particularly if ideological conviction is high. Consider Iran in 1979 or Pakistan in 2011, countries with a Westernized ruling class governing a young, poor population with little formal education and an attraction to what it sees as traditional Islamic virtues. Then divide that ruling class into those who believe that stability and progress requires firm, even authoritarian, leadership and those who believe that elected, representative governments represent the only way forward. In conditions such as these, it is not a question of whether the regime in power will be challenged, but of when and how.

Why did majority rule replace apartheid in South Africa when it did? As in most complex political events, no single explanation satisfies. But the loss of ideological conviction among the Afrikaner ruling class played a significant role. Apartheid's origins lay in the belief that God had given the Afrikaners both a gift—the land of South Africa—and a duty—to guide and rule the black African population of that land. It would be easy, but mistaken, to see this as simply a convenient justification for something the Afrikaner took and did simply because he had the power to do so. Generations of Afrikaners believed this, and therein lay the problem. You cannot negotiate on fundamentals with a person who believes that he is carrying out the will of God (or the will of the *Volk*, the Historical

Imperative, or whatever other supra-human cause animates the true believer). This belief system gradually eroded and with it went the Afrikaner ruling class's belief in its right to rule. Once that happened, negotiation became possible. The issues were still difficult, but now they were practical, not metaphysical. How could minority rights be assured in a political system based on majority rule? How could the Afrikaner be assured that he could keep his worldly goods? The analyst who failed to see the significance of this ideological change would also have failed to see the new opportunities that it created.

Distinguishing true from proclaimed ideology is a challenge for any diplomatic analyst, as is evaluating the extent to which relevant actors in the country's political system believe the ideology. There is no better way to do this than listening with a properly tuned ear to what people have to say and putting it into a broader context. In some countries, perhaps more often in authoritarian ones, a rich, sub-rosa tradition of political humor enlivens, lightens, and illuminates how the "man in the street" views developments in his country. At Embassy Moscow, our periodic synopses of political jokes had a widespread, virtually guaranteed and often high-level readership.

Often, a country's contemporary literature provides that broader context. In the late 1800s, Chekhov chronicled the ideological bankruptcy of Russia's ruling class. The issue for present purposes is not whether this was his primary intent, or for that matter any part of his intent. He eloquently and movingly portrayed a ruling class that lacked both belief in its right to rule and capacity to govern. His final play, *The Cherry Orchard,* is almost eerily prescient. The orchard, a metaphor for Russia's ruling class, or perhaps its values, is doomed. Its owner, Luba Andreyevna Ranevskaya, and her brother, Leonid Andreyevich Gayev, personify that ruling class. They can save themselves as individuals only by agreeing to sell the orchard, abandoning the values of their class. Incapable of that decision, they lose themselves in increasingly fanciful imaginings of how the orchard might be saved, as the day of its forced sale comes inexorably closer. The orchard is sold and lost, and they depart, Ranevskaya into foreign exile, Gayev to a banking job at which he is doomed to fail, listening as they leave to the axes beginning to fall on their beloved orchard's trees. The collapse of this ruling class was all but foreordained, although the timing and the trigger, the when and how, were not. It was doomed not by the professional revolutionaries, who had been forecasting its end for decades, but by its own internal decay. It might be argued, and cannot be denied, that a hundred or so years of hindsight inform this analysis. I would argue in return that with the aid of the correct analytical tools, the diplomatic craftsman of the early 1900s should have been able to arrive at the same conclusion.

CHANGE IS CONSTANT BUT NOT LINEAR

There is a tendency in all political analysis to extrapolate from the past into the future. This misses perhaps the most significant element in how societies evolve. Major social change follows a different path.

In *The Structure of Scientific Revolutions,* Thomas Kuhn invokes the concept of "paradigm shifts" to describe the process by which an existing tradition of scientific process is replaced by a new set of commitments, a new basis for the practice of science.[3] Essentially, Kuhn argues that an accepted scientific paradigm produces questions or puzzles that scientists seek to answer or solve. This question-answering or problem-solving scientific process Kuhn refers to as "normal science"—"a highly cumulative enterprise, eminently successful in its aim, the steady expansion of the scope and precision of scientific knowledge."[4] In carrying out normal science, its practitioners become aware of anomalies, aspects of nature that violate the expectations of the paradigm within which they are working. Scientists study these anomalies, seeking to reconcile them with the tenets of the paradigm. If they are unable to do so, the tenets themselves may be called into question, and the paradigm faces a crisis that may result in its replacement by a new paradigm. As Kuhn puts it:

> The transition from a paradigm in crisis to a new one from which a new tradition of normal science can emerge is far from a cumulative process, one achieved by an extension or articulation of the old paradigm. Rather, it is a reconstruction of the field from new fundamentals, a reconstruction that changes some of the field's most elementary theoretical generalizations as well as many of its paradigm methods and applications.[5]

Kuhn refers to these paradigm shifts as "scientific revolutions" and, recognizing that he has borrowed this vocabulary from the political realm, explicitly compares the processes of scientific and political revolutions.[6] We should return the favor and ask what his explanation of scientific revolutions can tell us about the process of political change in social structures.

Although he probably deliberately avoids the terminology, what Kuhn describes in *The Structure of Scientific Revolutions* is a dialectical process, not a linear one. Like Kuhn, I hesitate to introduce the term dialectics. Hegel is too heavy. Marx is too politically incorrect. And, in any case, Marxism has wound up on the scrap heap of history. Yet, considering political processes within a dialectical framework can be productive of understanding and insights that might otherwise be missed entirely. Those who cannot get their minds around dialectics should keep thinking 'paradigm shift' in the following discussion. Anticipating the anguish that this discussion will cause in philosophers and even more so in philosophy professors, I once again provide the caveat that this is a personal interpretation, an attempt to distill from several decades of experience a few tools that may help the diplomatic craftsman.

The historical dialectic asserts that since every society is inherently imperfect, each contains the seeds of its own destruction. These imperfections, or contradictions, accumulate quantitatively over time. At some point, the contradictions become so massive that they transmute from quantitative to qualitative. This sets the stage for a revolutionary change to a new social structure that reconciles the contradictions, after which the process recommences.

How does one know when the quantitative changes have become qualitative? This may be easier in the natural sphere than in the social. Gradually lower the temperature of water from 211 degrees Fahrenheit to 33 degrees. Through 178 degrees of temperature change, the water will have become progressively colder without any qualitative change in its physical appearance or texture. Lower it one more degree, and a qualitative change occurs. This type of qualitative change is easily understood, because it is tangible, physical. It can be seen and touched. Qualitative change is less easily identified in the social sphere, except in retrospect. One way of thinking about it is as the moment when the inconceivable becomes the possible. It is the moment in a difficult marriage when one of the spouses first thinks, "I do not have to go on this way"; the moment in a parent-child relationship when the child first realizes that the parent is fallible; the moment when the reformer comes to believe that the society is incapable of reform; the moment in a seemingly irreconcilable conflict when one side recognizes that it can be resolved. There is no inevitability to what happens after that moment, but there is also no way of looking once again at the future as one did before.

Societies change constantly because they are under constant pressure from forces that, by and large, cannot be controlled but must be adapted to: technology, demography, the international environment, and the society's own inherent inadequacies, to name but a few. Most of the time this change, this adaptation can be thought of as quantitative rather than qualitative. Indeed, it can be argued that the more successful societies are those that have institutionalized processes that allow adaptation to a wider range of challenges. But this limited, quantitative adaptation can fail. This may occur because a society that has adapted successfully to internal pressures faces an outside challenge beyond its capabilities. Indigenous societies in the Americas, even if previously successful, simply could not resist the overwhelming force of the European colonial conquests or the expansion of the United States westward. Alternatively, it may occur because the society has not adapted to those internal pressures and they have accumulated beyond its present ability to cope. The Soviet Union in the 1980s is a classic example of such a society.

The diplomatic craftsman, in most societies, most of the time, deals with quantitative change. That makes it easy to think of change as linear. It is a way of thinking that must be resisted, because it does not correspond to reality and will likely render him incapable of recognizing genuinely tectonic social shifts when they do occur. American embassies create annual Post Reporting Plans (PRPs), approved by the relevant geographic bureau at the State Department, in which they specify the significant analytical reports that they plan to produce during the calendar year and the planned dates of submission. The PRP is an excellent organizational and management tool, beautifully suited to paradigm exploration and ideal for a linearly evolving reality. It can also serve as the canary in the coal mine. If the topics of the PRP are regularly out of date before they can be researched, if the PRP needs constant revision to keep up with local reality, the reason could simply be a bad PRP, but it could also mark the onset of revolutionary change, of a shift in paradigms. We found this to be the case in Moscow during the latter years of the Gorbachev period.

Every society has its own paradigm, the set of basic tenets under which it operates. Understanding that paradigm allows the analyst to evaluate the underlying forces at work that support or challenge the existing paradigm. This allows him to put the specific events of everyday political life into an appropriate context, one of the fundamental objectives of political analysis.

THE VIOLENCE AND INTENSITY OF CONFLICT

Conflict is the engine of social change. The political analyst must understand the nature of conflict in a given society, how that society views conflict, and what its mechanisms are for managing it. Ralf Dahrendorf, the German sociologist, argues that conflict is inevitable in any group involving authority relations between the class made up of those who rule and the class made up of those who are ruled. Such conflicts vary along two principal dimensions: violence and intensity. The spectrum of violence involves the weapons used and ranges from peaceful discussion to warfare. Intensity refers to the energy expenditure and degree of involvement of the parties to the conflict. When the costs of victory or defeat are low, intensity tends also to be low and vice versa. Violence and intensity both affect the outcome of conflict but in different ways. The more violent the class conflict, the more sudden and complete the exchange of personnel in dominant positions. The more intense the class conflict, the more radical the change in the group's values and institutions.[7]

A society experiencing intense class conflict has much in common with a scientific paradigm in crisis. In both cases, fundamental beliefs about how the world is ordered are under challenge. Proponents of a new scientific theory may initially be greeted with hostility, perhaps even shunned and denied professional standing by those who adhere to the dominant existing paradigm. All that, and a lot worse, may be the fate of those seeking fundamental change in their societies.

If the ruling class has little ideological conviction—as is the case, for example, in many developing countries—conflict will often be violent, but it is rarely intense. A ruling cabal will be overthrown with as much or as little violence as is necessary to accomplish the task, but little else will change in the society as a whole. An entirely different situation arises, however, when tribal identity and ruling/subordinate class coincide. Tribal loyalty plays the same political role as ideological conviction. The intensity of conflict increases because the stakes are higher, as is the emotional involvement of the parties. A change of leadership now means a change in values with potentially much wider societal implications. Anyone with an interest in African history can cite numerous examples of both types of conflict, from the typical palace coup on one end to the Hutu-Tutsi tragedy in Rwanda at the other. Conflict is similarly intensified when religious conviction is superimposed on class conflict, as with the Sunni and the Shia in Iraq, or when ethnic and religious differences are superimposed on class conflict, as with the Serbs and the Bosnians in the former Yugoslavia.

These examples suggest that highly intense conflicts tend also to be highly violent. That is not necessarily the case. Intensity and violence are different dimensions of conflict. How they manifest themselves in a given society is a reflection of that society's structural ability to cope with conflict. The political analyst must assess that capability along both the violence and intensity dimensions.

IS THE POWER STRUCTURE RIGID, OR IS IT FLEXIBLE?
Societies differ greatly in their attitude toward conflict and in their ability and mechanisms for coping with it. Some societies deny the legitimacy of conflict; others attempt to institutionalize it. The authors of the American Constitution, distrusting power, created

competing institutions to limit it. They considered political conflict not only legitimate, but desirable. Tempering their personal religious beliefs with the Enlightenment values of reason and tolerance, they sought to create a set of political institutions that would be flexible enough to allow the expression of widely varying convictions and authoritative enough to prevent the imposition of any particular convictions.

How does one gauge the strength of a country's political institutions? I would suggest that they are strong if they have the power to limit the violence of conflict and the flexibility to limit its intensity. Both are important. It is easy to confuse rigidity with strength. Political or religious dissidents fortunate enough to be allowed to emigrate from the Soviet Union to the United States in the 1970s and early 1980s frequently made this mistake. They feared that the divisiveness and "weakness" that they saw in America's institutions would lead it to defeat in its contest with the Soviet Union. I could not convince the ones I knew that they were mistaking flexibility for weakness.

A rigid power structure appears strong but is actually fragile. It maintains power by its monopoly of the instruments of violence and by employing them actively to suppress conflict. It emphasizes stability and the rightness of its institutions, resists change, and denies the legitimacy of conflict. Its political, economic, military, religious, and intellectual elites tend to overlap, increasing its perceived strength. Conflict in such societies tends to be more intense than it is in more pluralistic societies, and change, when it does come, tends to be more radical.[8] Societies with a rigid power structure are subject to rapid and complete collapse, often with little immediate violence (although, historically, subsequent efforts by members of the ousted ruling class to regain power have led to extremely violent civil conflicts).

How is the political analyst to recognize when such change may occur? It may be too much to expect a satisfactory answer to the "when." There are simply too many variables, too many unknowns. But perhaps the analyst with the right tools may do a better job of recognizing that a qualitative social change has occurred, that the inconceivable has now become the possible. This involves understanding the fundamental forces at work in the society that support or challenge its ruling paradigm, its ideological structure. A society is, for example, in crisis when the ruling elite has lost its belief in its right to rule and when the ruled no longer believe it is able or willing to use force to impose its will. The more authoritarian such a society is, the more it is ripe for sudden, radical change.

Shortly after my arrival at Embassy Moscow, I took a Saturday morning stroll on one of the city's main streets, passing a small park containing a statue of Russia's great poet Alexander Pushkin, where a small human rights demonstration was under way. It had become a tradition in Moscow, dating back at least to the 1970s, for the city's human rights activists to attempt to mount demonstrations at this location once or twice a year. In the past, KGB operatives had vastly outnumbered the demonstrators and would engulf them as soon as their signs appeared. It would be over, and the demonstrators hauled away to waiting vehicles in minutes.

This occasion was different. Security personnel were on hand but had obviously been given orders not to interfere. The demonstration was proceeding peacefully. Hundreds of passersby were stopping to watch. I stood across the street among them. A uniformed policeman nearby was assertively trying to tell the passersby to move on, that there was nothing here they needed to see. Few left. Most reacted passively, simply moving back a little. Then I heard a man tell the officer that this was a Moscow street and that he had the right to stand on it wherever he wanted. Murmurs of assent emerged from the crowd. The policeman was at a loss. He was obviously under orders that precluded either arresting the man or beating him up. He gave up and drifted away.

I had on the same day for the first time seen a human rights demonstration proceed without interference and heard an ordinary Soviet citizen, not a political dissident, tell a security official that he had rights. I knew that this was significant, but I would not at that time have anticipated that within eighteen months hundreds of thousands of Soviet citizens would be demonstrating in the streets, or that within three years thousands of Soviet citizens would force a small group of reactionary leaders to choose between ordering the Red Army to open fire on them or watching their anti-reform coup collapse. I was witnessing the first stages of a fundamental paradigm shift. On one side, the ruling class no longer believed in its right to use violence indiscriminately to impose its will. On the other side, the ruled were coming to believe that they had some rights beyond those permitted them by the authorities.

PROBABILITY ANALYSIS OR RISK MANAGEMENT?

Probability analysis is an appropriate analytical tool, but risk management merits more significant use than it has gotten in the foreign policy community. Probability analysis essentially involves projecting current trend lines into the future. It is inherently linear. This is not necessarily a bad thing. Most societies at most times will not be on the cusp of paradigm shifts. Risk management should rely more heavily on nonlinear approaches. Its essential task is to limit the downside risks of alternative futures.

Predicting the most probable outcome is a relatively trivial task. Planning for its consequences, if the predicted outcome is benign or positive, does not require great forethought. High fives all around, pass the bottle, and promotions for all. On the other hand, a low-probability event, but one of enormous significance if it should occur, ought to engage the attention of a country's political leaders and the best thinking of their advisers with a view toward risk management. That has probably never been an easy task, but today's mass media have made it even harder. Corporations, often criticized for their focus on the quarterly report, are strategic thinkers of the first order compared to some political leaders and their advisers, who become mesmerized by the daily press briefing.

An outcome whose probability is so small as to be in effect inconceivable is not worth spending time and attention on. The conceptual leap from inconceivable to low probability is qualitative, not quantitative. During the Cold War, the collapse of the Soviet Union seemed either inconceivable or so historically distant a possibility as to be irrelevant for present purposes. After the collapse, of course, there was no shortage of analysts explaining why it was inevitable. While such analyses are appropriate and can even be useful, collectively they create the impression that a qualitative, revolutionary step was simply the final event in a linear, cumulative history.[9] Future analysts, who did not personally experience the drama of the events in question, will tend to accept this linear view, locking themselves into an intellectual paradigm that will inhibit their ability to understand future fundamental changes. After-the-fact deconstructions of revolutions often conclude that they were inevitable. They erect signposts toward the revolution, thereby reinforcing the tendency to see the process as linear. But where were the signposts before the revolution? And why do those signposts so rarely point toward the next? It is because the signposts lead not to the event, but to the conceptual chasm that must be leaped. Linearity cannot make that leap.[10]

When exiled Soviet dissident Andrei Amalrik asked in his 1970 book *Will the Soviet Union Last until 1984?*, he made the conceptual leap from inconceivable to possible, as, separately, did Bernard Levin in 1977. Both understood that the forces already at work in Soviet society, prominent among them rising nationalism in the Soviet republics, could threaten the empire's existence, not in some future generation, but in the historical present.[11]

Risk management can, and has been, misused to justify higher defense and intelligence budgets by making worst-case assumptions the basis for strategic planning. Properly used, it can help mitigate the impact even of bad policy choices. It was not, for example, inconceivable that Saddam Hussein's Iraq had no weapons of mass destruction and it was far from inconceivable that the Iraqi political culture would not immediately be fertile ground for Western-style democratic values, the latter a conclusion reached by an intelligence community assessment shortly before the war.[12] A risk management team prepared to assess the consequences of less desirable outcomes might not have changed the decision of an administration determined to go to war, but it might have enabled better planning for the way events actually unfolded.

One problem, which we discuss further in a later chapter, is that leaders may not want analysis of politically sensitive subjects, lest the results contradict their preferences and become public knowledge. While "red teams" are sometimes used to challenge intelligence community analyses by playing devil's advocate, the sad fact is that they are more likely to be used to challenge findings that contradict the views of the political leadership than the reverse.[13] An earlier experiment with competitive analysis, that of George H.W. Bush during his term as CIA director became, in one observer's view, "a lesson in unintended consequences, as the team of outside experts brought their own set of decidedly hawkish biases that ultimately appeared to politicize the original (CIA Analyst's) estimates." This led the Carter administration to sideline competitive analysis, "but the unintended consequence of that reform was a more ad hoc, bureaucratically fractured, and less authoritative set of judgments."[14] Risk management is not a panacea, but, properly used, it can be a highly useful analytical and planning tool. This is an area in which embassy dispatches can play a key role, if they are allowed and encouraged to remain separate from "inside the Beltway" political pressures, a subject to which we shall return in the final chapter.

ANALYTICAL TOOLS THAT ARE COUNTRY SPECIFIC
Political Culture

We have discussed cultural understanding above as one of the diplomatic political analyst's personal tools. The present discussion narrows the focus to political culture. In chapter 1, we defined political analysis as "the attempt to convey an understanding of how authority and power relations are operating and evolving within and between governments and between government and society." In attempting to convey that understanding, the analyst needs to understand how fundamental cultural values shape authority and power relations. He must also understand that the putative or official values may not be the real ones and that the values that shape popular political culture may not be the same as those that shape the political culture of the ruling class. In distinguishing between the official, dominant, and elite political cultures, one noted student of the subject defines the dominant as "subjective perceptions of history and politics, fundamental political beliefs and values, foci of identification and loyalty, and political knowledge and expectations."[15]

An ideology operates within a political culture. It is not identical to it, nor does it supersede it. To be successful, an ideology must correspond in fundamental ways to the values of the relevant political culture. Much of Lenin's genius lay in his adaptation of Marxism to the Russian political culture. He knew, at a level deeper than intellectual understanding, that authoritarianism and risk-avoidance were that culture's dominant elements. It was no accident that Marxism-Leninism, and not simply Marxism, formed the ideological base of Russia's political elite during the Soviet Union's formative years.

Genuine understanding of a country's political culture allows the analyst to see past the events of the day and helps establish the boundaries of what they mean. For example, understanding that authoritarianism and risk-avoidance dominate Russian political culture[16] does not guarantee accurate analysis, but failing to understand it all but guarantees inaccurate analysis. One would be hard put to find a more compelling example of this than the trajectory of Russia's political life since the collapse of the Soviet Union in 1991.

Many supposedly knowledgeable Western observers saw a triumph of democratic and capitalist values in Russia under Boris Yeltsin. Western democratic values are not part of the Russian political culture, and it was remarkably naïve to believe that they would have been internalized so quickly. Where Westerners were seeing democracy, Russians were seeing anarchy and economic collapse. Where those same Western observers saw growing authoritarianism in Russia during Vladimir Putin's time in office, Russians saw a return to order and economic growth. The state often could not pay wages and pensions during the Yeltsin years; under Putin, aided, of course, by high oil prices, it paid them on time and raised them significantly. Given a choice between a situation that they see as anarchic and one they see as authoritarian, it is quite predictable that Russians will choose the more authoritarian. Given an association of Western democratic values with perceived anarchy and economic collapse, it is quite predictable that Russians will have little admiration for Western democratic values.

It is not surprising that Putin was wildly popular during his two terms as president and, at this writing, remains so as premier. Events since 1991 have reinforced the core values of traditional Russian political culture, not weakened or changed them. In the midst of a severe economic downturn in January 2009, 61 percent of respondents responding to a poll on the main threats facing Russia indicated inflation and unemployment. Far down on the list were arbitrary government (8 percent) and government incompetence (7 percent), although corruption and bureaucracy, often seen as virtually one and the same by Russians, were cited by 41 percent of respondents.[17] Any poll is only a snapshot, and one would expect economic concerns to dominate a period of economic difficulty. Nevertheless, these results are consistent with a traditional Russian tendency to separate the "bad" bureaucracy from the "good" government (or tsar), and to blame the former for the country's troubles. Events of the past twenty years have demonstrated, however, that personal popularity in Russia can plummet extraordinarily quickly. The Russian political structure has become more rigid, as well as more authoritarian, in recent years, its ruling class lacks a clear ideological base to justify its right to rule, and the ability of both structure and class to adapt sufficiently to withstand the challenges of an extended economic downturn is open to question.

The diplomatic analyst needs to determine whether a single political culture is dominant in the country, or whether there are a number of political cultures, either competing or coexisting. Prior to the breakup of Yugoslavia, for example, an analyst might have concluded that ethnic and religious differences had produced several political cultures within the country, each dominant in a particular area and each different from the official, Titoist values. Understanding the core values and beliefs of the political culture allows the analyst to put day-to-day events into a framework that has greater meaning.

Personality and Charisma

Much of the previous discussion assumes that if the craftsman brings the right tools to bear, he can understand political processes because they do not operate randomly. There are, however, also some wild cards in the political deck. Charisma is one of them. Can any dictionary definition do adequate justice to charisma? It is that "something" that causes otherwise rational men and women to follow another person down a path that is not of their choosing, that may not be in their self-interest, and that in some cases appears to descend inevitably toward their ruin or death. The charismatic individual embodies an ideology, which he may or may not have created. He has an instinct for the emotional jugular of his audience. In virtuous hands, charisma can do great good. In other hands, it can do even greater harm. Mikhail Gorbachev was not charismatic. His Russian was too provincial for the intelligentsia. The working class would have forgiven him for that, but he was too cold and cerebral for them. Boris Yeltsin, at least for a time, had charisma. He was not intellectual and could, at times, be remarkably uncouth, but this had no bearing. He stood up to power in a way that Russians admired, even if they could not, or perhaps because they would not, emulate it. A female Russian lawyer in 1990 described him to me as a "saint." I remarked on his reputation for drinking and womanizing. She dismissed this as something that all men did. It had no bearing on Boris's sainthood. He had a remarkably rapid fall from grace, but that is another matter.

Power contributes to an impression of charisma but does not ensure it. Charisma may lead to power but does not guarantee it. George W. Bush had considerable power, at least during the first six years of his presidency, despite razor-thin election victories, because he asserted it and had a generally compliant majority from his political party in the legislature. But few would name charisma among his attributes. Bill Clinton had some charisma, but, like Boris Yeltsin, also brought ultimately crippling weaknesses to the table.

Some societies have a weakness for charismatic leaders; others distrust them. Recent experience with a charismatic leader who led to disaster is likely to lead, at least in the short run, to a preference for a more mundane personality, an apparatchik rather than a rock star. It is tempting to hypothesize that societies in ideological crisis are ripe for the emergence of a charismatic leader, one who can articulate a new social paradigm and bring an end to the intellectual discomfort that results from a collapse of accepted values.

Diplomatic political analysis is often too person-focused. In part this is because it mirrors the focus of high-level policymakers, who tend to overestimate the importance of their individual contacts with other leaders and to underestimate that of the underlying forces that are not under their control. That said, there is no excuse for not knowing as much as possible about the political views, motivations, aspirations, and personalities of key individuals in the national political process. Particularly during periods of intense social conflict, when the fundamental values of the society are in dispute, the direction in which the society will go may well depend on the values of competing aspirants for power. What direction would the Russian Revolution have taken without Lenin? Germany in the 1930s without Hitler? The Soviet Union in the 1980s without Gorbachev? We cannot answer those questions except with speculation. We can, however, say that each of these countries was in a crisis sufficiently grave to produce a paradigmatic shift in its values. At that tipping point, the values of the victorious leader played a far greater role in the future direction of his society than they would have if that same leader had aspired to power at a different point in his country's history.

CHAPTER SEVEN

CRITERIA FOR SUPERIOR REPORTING
The State Department View

The director general of the Foreign Service annually gives an award generally known in the State Department as the political reporting award. Its current formal title is the Director General's Award for Originality and Creativity in Reporting. In an average year, perhaps two dozen nominations are submitted. Normally, only one person receives the award, although occasionally two winners have been named. The recipient survives two exacting peer reviews. The first takes place at his diplomatic post, where his superiors must decide that the quality of his work merits a nomination and, further, that it stands out sufficiently from the work of his colleagues at the post that he should be singled out with the nomination. The latter hurdle may be higher than the former. The second peer review occurs when his work is compared by the award committee with that of the other nominees.

This seems as objective a place as one can readily find to look for the criteria that the State Department considers important in political analysis. The information below comes primarily from the State Department's monthly magazine, *State*, supplemented by responses from several recipients of the award to a questionnaire. I had hoped when I began the research for this book in 2007 to review some of the original, unclassified nomination documents, but the director general's office declined to make them available, advised me to file a Freedom of Information Act request to obtain them, and then informed me that it had destroyed the very documents it had told me to file the Freedom of Information Act request to obtain. Franz Kafka, or perhaps Joseph Heller, could no doubt better explain than I can why a bureaucracy would go to such devious lengths to ensure that its more admirable work be hidden from the public eye.[1]

GEOGRAPHIC FACTORS

State magazine provided information on twenty award winners for the period 1984–2007.[2] Some areas of the world were far more likely to produce winners than others. Reporting officers from sub-Saharan Africa and South America each received one award; by contrast, those from the Middle East received eight, or 40 percent of the total awards. One might suppose that this disparity arises from the fact that the Middle East is a perennial point of tension in the world and regularly on the front pages of major newspapers. This may have played some role but not a conclusive one. Although this period included the dissolution of the Warsaw Pact, the collapse of the Soviet Union and the economic and political reform process in Eastern Europe and the former Soviet Union, only one reporting officer from this region received the award, a nominee from Moscow in 1996. No region of the world, except for the Middle East, produced more than three award winners during this period.

I suspect that three factors produced the tilt toward Middle Eastern awardees during this period. The first is the previously mentioned prominence of Middle Eastern issues combined with the political complexity of the domestic and international issues involved. Second, the region may attract more than its share of the more talented Foreign Service officers. In fact, during my tenure at State, the Bureau for Middle Eastern Affairs had the "corridor reputation" of consistently being at or near the top of the department's bureaucracy in terms of management and talent. Finally, success may beget success. Supervisors in the region, conscious of previous award success, may be far more likely to nominate talented political officers than supervisors in other areas of the world.

THE CRITERIA

An article in *State* magazine in 1987 listed the following criteria for exemplary reporting:

- Sources
- Organization
- Relevance
- Analytic and interpretive content
- Overall usefulness[3]

A careful review of the *State* articles summarizing the criteria cited by the awards committee for the winners' selection indicated some overlap with the criteria above and some differences. In descending order of frequency, the committee cited:

- Usefulness (twenty-five mentions)
- Analytic and interpretive content (thirteen mentions)
- Sources and contacts (eleven mentions)
- Style (ten mentions)
- Cultural and linguistic skills (four mentions)
- Groundbreaking content (four mentions)

An obvious question arises. How are the criteria defined and distinguished from one another, either in the 1987 article or in the award citations? In fact, they are not, which introduces considerable subjectivity into the process. Most Foreign Service officers would not have difficulty agreeing on what constitutes good sources and contacts, or superior cultural and linguistic skills. They would probably agree that they would recognize an effective and pleasing writing style when they saw it. However, getting them to agree on what constitutes usefulness in reporting and how analytical and interpretive, or groundbreaking content are defined would be far more challenging. Many would probably argue that good sources and contacts are not possible without superior cultural and linguistic skills, and that superior cultural and linguistic skills without good sources and contacts are irrelevant. The reporting awards only partly support this belief. Although three of the four awardees cited for their cultural and linguistic skills were also cited for their sources and contacts, in eight cases sources and contacts received mention as factors, but cultural and linguistic skills did not. The materials available on this issue raise perhaps a more interesting question. In only one award since 1996 were sources and contacts mentioned; the last mention of cultural and linguistic skills was in 1997. This may be an artifact of the data. If not, it would appear that perceptions in Washington about what constitute the most important strengths of embassy reporting are changing.

THE KEY COMPONENT: USEFULNESS

It would be hard to argue with the contention that superior diplomatic reporting should be useful. Agreeing on what constitutes usefulness might well be another matter. One recipient of the award defines usefulness as "providing information and analysis that is (1) relevant to ongoing policy issues and (2) easily understood/accessible to the reader."[4] The award citations appear to identify four facets of usefulness:

- Timeliness
- Relevance to U.S. interests

- Aid to policymakers
- Predictive accuracy

The fact that the awards committee cited fifteen of the twenty recipients reviewed here for their assistance to policymakers seems to put that criterion in a special category, as perhaps it should be. The qualities of timeliness, relevance, and predictive accuracy, each mentioned three or four times in the twenty award citations can perhaps be thought of as necessary but not sufficient conditions for usefulness. It is tempting even to consider usefulness and aid to policymakers as one and the same. After all, the role of the Foreign Service, and of Foreign Service reporting, is to provide advice and assistance to the levels of government that make decisions about foreign policy. Further reflection suggests, however, that the two should not be confounded. A key role that embassy reporting can play is to provide a healthy dose of local reality to challenge Washington-based preconceptions. Such reporting may be incredibly useful, but will it be seen in Washington as an aid to policymakers? Set aside whether it *should* be so seen. In my experience, only the exceptional policymaker will be as open to views that challenge his own as to those that support it. Steven Kashkett, a career Foreign Service officer who received the Director General's Award in 1992, had this to say in 2008:

> The most serious obstacle to effective embassy reporting over the past few years has been the decline of truly candid analysis and the pervasive sense among political officers overseas that their analytical judgments are unwelcome in Washington, especially when [those judgments] call into question the conventional wisdom or the administration's preconceived foreign policy in a particular area."[5]

The public information available is not sufficient to permit us to determine how reporting awards are divided between analyses that support policies already in place and analyses that in effect critique those policies. We can say that the importance of predictive accuracy as a necessary precondition for usefulness appears to have declined over time. It has not been mentioned in an award citation since 1997. Timeliness and relevance, although mentioned no more frequently overall than predictive accuracy, have continued to be cited in this decade. Award committees have always supported reporting that aids policymakers, as evidenced by the fact that it is the most frequently cited single reason for granting an award. There appears to be a slight but not conclusive trend toward singling out that criterion more frequently in this decade than in the 1990s. When asked what they personally considered the chief merits of the reports for which they received nominations for the Director General's Award, two recipients of the award responded as follows:

> First, they were timely; that is, they involved issues on Washington's agenda and which were of interest or concern to policymakers. Second, they were well sourced and reflected in a concise and readable way the variety of opinion and analysis we were hearing from Israelis. Third, they added some policy value; i.e., they either suggested ways to deal with vexing issues or laid out choices in a stark enough manner for policymakers to understand the implications of choosing different options. And, fourth, they were readable and relatively concise.[6]

Substantively, the reports benefitted from intense interest at the highest levels in the substance—they fit into the administration's Middle East peace efforts. In dealing with the substance, the reports tried to provide a framework for understanding what was going on and, just as important, for evaluating what would develop going forward. I wanted them to be a lens through which to view the daily spot reports and news headlines. In addition, the reports demonstrated an "inside out" view of what key Palestinian leaders were thinking that I hoped would set them apart from the press and other diplomatic reporting. Stylistically and structurally, the reports had strong summary and comment paragraphs, so a busy person could quickly get the meat of the cables. I think they also benefitted from a strong story line and detailed quotes/facts, so that they could be lifted almost whole into memos and intelligence reports. Finally, they were short enough that they could be read.[7]

Examples

I had hoped to present a number of different examples of reports that had been selected as among the best that embassies have produced over the last twenty years, but the difficulties mentioned above in accessing the department's nominations imposed limits. Fortunately for the purposes of this book, Kashkett provided the cable numbers for two of the principal reports that provided the basis for his nomination by the consul general in Jerusalem. With that specific information, I was able to request and obtain declassification of the cables using the publicly available department procedures for doing so. The cables are presented below. The signatory, "Williamson," was consul general at the time and the highest-ranking officer at the post. Reports from U.S. diplomatic missions are always sent out signed by the highest-ranking officer, rather than signed by the report's author. A few sections have been excised by the department, apparently to protect the identities of specific sources cited. This accords with standard practice and seems to me to have been entirely appropriate. The excisions do not appear to affect the substance of the reports.

EXAMPLE 1: ARABS AND JEWS IN "REUNITED" JERUSALEM

CONFIDENTIAL
JERUSALEM 02228
R 101130Z JUN 92
FM AMCONSUL JERUSALEM
TO SECSTATE WASHDC 7623
INFO ARAB ISRAELI COLLECTIVE
CONFIDENTIAL JERUSALEM 02228
E.O. 12356: DECL:OADR
TAGS: PBTS, PGOV, KPAL, PHUM, IS, US
SUBJECT: ARABS AND JEWS IN "REUNITED" JERUSALEM: A TALE
OF TWO CITIES

1. CONFIDENTIAL — ENTIRE TEXT.
SUMMARY
2. Jerusalem, 25 years after its "reunification" under Israeli control, remains a bitterly divided city. While Israelis this week celebrate the anniversary of their 1967 victory, Palestinian Jerusalemites bemoan what they perceive as an ever-worsening disaster. Although the "green line" — the former border separating the Israeli and Jordanian sectors — has been blurred by the construction of huge Jewish settlement neighborhoods in East Jerusalem, the two communities still live in different, largely segregated worlds that share only a deep hostility towards each other. The disparities between Arab and Jewish Jerusalem are as great as ever.
3. Israelis see the past 25 years as a success story, their return to the ancient city of David and the consolidation of Jerusalem as capital of the state of Israel. They point with pride to the growth of the Jewish population throughout the municipality, the proliferation of new roads, parks, and

schools in their neighborhoods, the protection of the holy sites, and the development of Jerusalem as an international tourist center. Few Israelis ever enter the Arab quarters of town or concern themselves with the problems of East Jerusalem. Nonetheless, Mayor Teddy Kollek holds up his city as a model of peaceful coexistence between Arabs and Jews.

4. Palestinian Jerusalemites, on the other hand, remain outsiders even after 25 years of Israeli annexation. Most profess loyalty to the PLO, consider East Jerusalem to be the capital of their homeland, and reject Israeli sovereignty. They feel abused and disenfranchised by the Israeli government and Kollek's municipality. Although many of them have enjoyed certain advantages of living under Israeli law, few avail themselves of the right to apply for Israeli citizenship or to vote in city elections. At the height of the Intifada, many East Jerusalem Arab neighborhoods exploded in violent demonstrations comparable to those in West Bank towns and villages. Today, heavily-armed border police units control Arab areas of the city and treat Arab residents little differently from West Bankers.

5. Despite high-toned rhetoric, both the GOI and the municipality have for 25 years neglected Arab Jerusalem's needs and suppressed its growth. In sharp contrast to Israeli residential areas, Arab neighborhoods are decrepit places completely lacking in the infrastructure that the government has lavished on Jewish neighborhoods. They have few paved roads, sidewalks, sewers, public parks, or playgrounds. Although Arab residents pay high taxes, they suffer from a near-total absence of public services such as road maintenance, garbage collection, public transportation, mail delivery, and adequate schooling. Israeli authorities have expropriated vast tracts of Arab-owned land and financed the construction of massive Jewish settlement neighborhoods — to further the explicitly-defined "Judaization" of East Jerusalem — yet have made it very difficult for Palestinian families to get building permits.

6. The two communities see the future in opposite terms. The Israeli Jerusalemites look forward to the planned construction of major housing projects, shopping complexes, museums, and a convention center on the Jewish side of town. In spite of international disapprobation, Israelis rest secure in the knowledge that a "national consensus" favors retaining all of Jerusalem as Israel's "eternal capital" and reinforcing its Jewish majority.

Palestinians, by contrast, fear that their future in Jerusalem is being eroded daily. For them, the drive to increase Jewish settlement in East Jerusalem forebodes the continuing expropriation of Arab-owned land and the simultaneous restriction of growth and development in the Arab sector. Most of all, they dread an acceleration of the Likud-sponsored takeovers of houses in existing Arab neighborhoods by militant Jewish settlement groups. At least for the foreseeable future, "reunited" Jerusalem is likely to remain a tale of two cities.

END SUMMARY

STILL DIVIDED AFTER ALL THESE YEARS

7.   Israeli and Palestinian residents of Jerusalem reacted very differently to the commemoration of "Jerusalem Day" last week, marking the 25th anniversary since Israel's victory over Jordanian forces in 1967 and its subsequent annexation of the eastern part of the city. Israeli terminology — "reunification" rather than annexation — obscures the fact that Jerusalem today remains a bitterly divided city. The celebration along one side of town paralleled the despair on the other.

8.   Mayor Teddy Kollek and the city government that he controls have had only limited success since 1967 in erasing the "Green Line", the former boundary between the Israeli and Jordanian sectors. The barbed wire, minefields, and sniper posts along the Green Line are gone, but the mentality remains. A de facto segregation persists between the two halves of the city; with very few exceptions, neighborhoods are either exclusively Jewish or exclusively Arab. Moreover, both sides view the other as alien and menacing. Palestinians rarely venture into Rehavia, Har Nof, or Beit Hakerem, and few Israelis dare to set foot in Al-Ayzariyah, Shu'Fat, or Jebel Mukaber. The divided-city mentality is so pervasive that Congenoffs [consul general officers] are constantly forced to explain to both Israelis and Palestinians that the consulate, which has one building on the east side and one on the west side, is not two separate missions.

9.   Despite 25 years of coexistence in the "reunited" city, Palestinian and Israeli Jerusalemites live in separate worlds with little interaction between them. Even the huge, well-manicured Jewish settlement neighborhoods that have sprung up with massive government financing in many parts of East Jerusalem–i.e., across the Green Line — avoid all contact with the

run-down, underdeveloped Arab neighborhoods nearby. The economic, social, and political disparities between Arab and Jewish Jerusalem are as great as ever.

10. For historical reasons, Israelis are bound to see their past 25 years in Jerusalem as a success. All other factors, from the Israeli point of view, pale in significance next to the accomplishment of consolidating the return to the ancient city of David and its reinforcement as the capital of the state. Memories of the Jordanian desecration of Jewish holy sites between 1948 and 1967, including the Western Wall and the Hebrew Cemetery on the Mount of Olives, and the razing of the Jewish quarter of the Old City still strike a deep chord of bitterness among Israelis. The assertion of Israeli control over East Jerusalem has made possible the preservation of these holy sites and the reconstruction of the Jewish quarter.

11. City officials point with pride to a variety of other achievements. Christian and Muslim holy sites, they note, are protected places under Israeli law, and access to them is guaranteed. Mayor Kollek contends that, with the exception of a short period during the Intifada, Jerusalem under his stewardship has flourished as an international city and as a major tourist center. Museums and other cultural attractions have mushroomed since 1967. The Jerusalem Foundation, a non-profit fundraising organization that works closely with the municipality, sponsors hundreds of social and cultural projects for the benefit of city residents (a handful of these are located in East Jerusalem).

12. The tripling of the Jewish population throughout the municipality since 1967 is a basic element of the Jerusalem success story, in Israeli eyes, because the "Judaization" of the city is a fundamental, stated policy goal. Even though Jerusalem has undergone a flight of secular residents over the past decade, it has steadily increased its overall Jewish population, now close to half a million, through the influx and propagation of ultra-Orthodox families and through the arrival of new immigrants. Some 140,000 Israelis today live in settlement neighborhoods in the eastern, formerly Jordanian sector, and another 25,000 in West Bank commuter settlements immediately adjacent to Jerusalem.

13. Israeli Jerusalemites cite as part of the success story the proliferation of new roads, parks, and schools in their neighborhoods, many of which are

attractive garden communities. Despite its slightly lower per capita income, Jerusalem is a much more beautiful, more livable city than any other large Israeli town. City officials argue that, since its "reunification", Jerusalem has been transformed from a neglected backwater into a world-class capital; one of their great frustrations is the refusal of foreign governments to recognize it as such.

14. Most importantly, in spite of the animosities cited earlier, the Mayor continues to hold up Jerusalem as a model of peaceful coexistence between Arabs and Jews. Teddy Kollek's international reputation is based more on his perceived efforts to achieve this harmony between the two halves of the city than on any other factor. Israelis generally accept wholeheartedly this supposition, even though few ever enter the Arab quarters of town or concern themselves with the problems of East Jerusalem.

ALIENATION ON THE ARAB SIDE

15. Palestinian Jerusalemites, on the other hand, remain outsiders even after living for 25 years under Israeli annexation. Most Arab residents consider East Jerusalem to be the capital of their homeland and therefore reject Israeli sovereignty over it. Many disdainfully refer to Mayor Kollek's administration as the "West Jerusalem municipality". Some have enjoyed certain advantages of living under Israeli law, such as the ability to bring issues before the civil courts, the freedom to travel without restrictions, and the opportunity to attend Israeli universities. Nonetheless, few avail themselves of the right to apply for Israeli citizenship or to vote in city elections.

16. Traditional East Jerusalem leaders such as Feisal Husseini remain in the forefront of Palestinian nationalist activity in the occupied territories. The PLO commands the loyalty of most of the city's Palestinians, but Hamas is reportedly also strong in certain areas. The walls of East Jerusalem neighborhoods are covered with militant nationalist and Islamic fundamentalist graffiti and occasionally even the outlawed Palestinian flag. At the height of the Intifada, many Arab neighborhoods exploded in violent demonstrations comparable to those in West Bank towns and villages. Today, heavily-armed border police units patrol Arab areas of the city and treat Arab residents little differently from West Bankers.

17. Twenty-five years of annexation have not lessened the sense of alienation

among Palestinian Jerusalemites. They feel abused and disenfranchised by the Israeli government and the municipality. Nowhere is this phenomenon more evident than in the treatment of Arab neighborhoods and the expropriation of Arab land for Jewish settlements in East Jerusalem.

THE OTHER SIDE OF THE TRACKS

18. Israeli officials over the years since 1967 have repeatedly stressed that all residents of "reunited" Jerusalem are treated equally, and the cornerstone of Mayor Kollek's international reputation is his role as staunch defender of the rights of Arab residents. Regardless of this stated policy, both the Israeli government and the Jerusalem municipality have for 25 years neglected the needs of the Arab population and suppressed its growth. The contrast between the condition of Jewish and Arab neighborhoods today is striking.

19. Over the past three months, Congenoff, in the company of Palestinian leaders and city officials, extensively surveyed Jerusalem's residential areas and observed these graphic disparities. Arab neighborhoods, with few exceptions, are decrepit places completely lacking in the infrastructure that the GOI and municipal government have lavished on Jewish areas. Many Palestinian homes can still only be reached by dirt roads. Arab neighborhoods have no street signs, no sidewalks, no sewers, no public parks, and no playgrounds. In contrast, Jewish residential quarters of West Jerusalem and settlement neighborhoods in East Jerusalem all boast well-paved, well-marked, well-lit roads with proper underground sewage and drainage pipes. Each Jewish neighborhood contains parks and playgrounds that were planned and financed by the Jerusalem municipality or the Jerusalem Foundation.

20. Palestinian residential areas suffer from a near-total absence of public services. Road maintenance is minimal, and thus many roads are pocked with potholes and erosion. Garbage collection in some neighborhoods is infrequent or non-existent; residents dump trash on vacant lots. Public transportation runs along a few main thoroughfares but enters almost no Arab neighborhoods. There is no door-to-door postal delivery in Arab areas, so mail must be picked up from the central East Jerusalem post office. The city has built few schools for Arab residents, so many Palestinians send their children either to private schools or to distant public schools in other neighborhoods. By contrast, every Jewish neighborhood

gets prompt road repairs, twice or thrice weekly garbage collection, regular bus service throughout the interior of the neighborhood, daily mail delivery, and the complete range of government-funded public and religious schools.

21. The most obvious disparity between Arab and Jewish neighborhoods can be seen in the area of new construction. According to the Jerusalem Institute for Israel Studies some 63,300 new housing units have been built for Israeli Jerusalemites since 1967, but only 8600 in Arab areas. Furthermore, over half of the Jewish residential construction was publicly financed, as compared to less than 6% for new Arab housing. In other words, the GOI paid for the infrastructure and financed most of the housing in every Jewish settlement neighborhood in East Jerusalem — a total of nearly 30,000 units — but since 1967 has sponsored the construction of only a few hundred dwellings in Arab neighborhoods.

22. Moreover, Palestinians are routinely denied permits to build new houses at their own expense. An official of the Arab neighborhood of Beit Hanina (pop. 15,000) told Congenoff that perhaps 50 permits had been granted for new home construction there over the past five years, although hundreds had been requested. Similar statistics abound in other Palestinian sections of Jerusalem, such as Jebel Mukaber, where local officials insist that fewer than a dozen new building permits are issued each year for a population of 13,000. In contrast, a settlement neighborhood of Pisgat Ze'ev, which abuts Beit Hanina, received 600 permits for new dwellings in one week earlier this year. Over 3500 new apartments are currently approaching completion in Pisgat Ze'ev.

23. Finally, Palestinians chafe at the knowledge that, while they are denied the right to build new homes, their land is being taken for the construction of Israeli settlement neighborhoods. Vast tracts of East Jerusalem land owned and registered by Palestinian families were expropriated for "public purpose" in the years following 1967. Construction of Jewish communities on these lands is then justified on the grounds that the "Judaization" of East Jerusalem is a "public purpose".

THE MUNICIPALITY'S RESPONSE

24. City officials do not deny these inequities but cite a variety of explanations for them. Both left-wing and right-wing municipal council members

accuse Mayor Kollek of deliberately focusing all of the city's resources and energies on the Jewish sections at the expense of the Arabs. Members of the Mayor's "One Jerusalem" party in turn blame the Israeli government, which is responsible for building most of the basic infrastructure that Arab neighborhoods lack. Although Israeli Jerusalemites point out that the government installed the first roads and street lighting ever in some Arab areas shortly after 1967, few disagree that the GOI since Likud's accession to power in 1967 has paid little attention to the physical needs of the city's Palestinian inhabitants.

25. Jerusalem officials invoke different reasons for the absence of services in Arab areas for which the municipality itself is responsible. [Name redacted] claimed to Congenoff that Palestinian neighborhoods receive fewer services because they pay less municipal tax. Palestinian leaders and left-wing city council members contest this claim. Most Arab areas, they admit, fall into lower tax brackets for the "arnona" (municipal tax) than do upper-scale Jewish neighborhoods, so Arab homeowners and businesses tend to pay a lower tax rate. This is counterbalanced, however, by the fact that the arnona is based on the size of a house; since Arab residences tend to be much larger than Israeli dwellings, Arabs are taxed for a higher number of square meters. [Name and title redacted], Arab Beit Hanina, estimates that his community's 15,000 residents pay at least 5 million shekels (dols 2 million) in arnona per year, but Beit Hanina receives practically nothing in municipal services.

26. [Name redacted] and others counter that the Intifada made it impossible for the municipality to provide many services in Arab areas. Streetlights, for example, are repeatedly smashed by local youths, and the city refuses to keep replacing them. Garbage collection in some neighborhoods, according to [name and title redacted] has become perilous since the beginning of the Intifada. Public transportation, asserts [name redacted], cannot realistically be extended into Arab areas until the safety of public buses is guaranteed (and until the government agrees to build proper two-lane roads in the interior of these neighborhoods). Few of these services, however, were available even before the Intifada.

27. [Name and title redacted] told CG [Consul General] that the municipality usually denies Palestinian requests for building permits on the grounds that

the land is not zoned for residential dwellings. He lamented that the lack of approved master plans for most Arab neighborhoods in East Jerusalem makes it impossible to determine proper zoning. [Name redacted] admits, however, that the municipality itself is responsible for drawing up such master plans, yet city planners only initiated the process 10 years ago. Moreover, in each case where a master plan has been approved for an Arab neighborhood, it sharply narrows the area in which residential construction is allowed. This process, known as "restrictive zoning", has placed off-limits most available land surrounding Palestinian neighborhoods by zoning them as "green" areas or as "public use" areas.

28. Despite all of the high-toned rhetoric and the multitude of justifications from city officials, it is difficult to escape the conclusion that Arab Jerusalem has been systematically shortchanged. There can be little doubt that Palestinian Jerusalemites have suffered from their own collective refusal to participate in municipal elections for the past 25 years. Resources in any city are allocated on the basis of political clout, and Jerusalem's Arab residents have none because they have chosen for symbolic reasons to boycott the process. Nonetheless, the official neglect of Arab interests in Jerusalem over the past 25 years belies the oft-cited ideal of a "reunited" city in which Israelis and Palestinians live in harmony.

OPPOSITE VISIONS OF THE FUTURE

29. Israeli Jerusalemites see bright prospects for the city. Municipal officials and Israeli residents look forward to the planned construction of major housing projects, shopping complexes, museums, government offices, a new zoo, and an international convention center — all on the Jewish side of town. They speak proudly and confidently of the city's future in spite of international disapprobation. As Israeli Jerusalemites ceaselessly remind Congenoff, a "national consensus" favors retaining all of Jerusalem as Israel's eternal capital and reinforcing its Jewish majority.

30. Palestinians, by contrast, fear that their future in Jerusalem is being eroded daily. From their perspective, the drive to increase Jewish settlement in East Jerusalem forebodes a continuation of the Israeli practice of expropriating Arab-owned land while simultaneously restricting growth and development in the Arab sector. Most of all, they dread an acceleration of the Likud-sponsored takeovers of houses in existing Arab neighborhoods by militant

Jewish settlement groups. As the likelihood grows that the post-Kollek municipal government will be dominated by Likud right-wingers and religious parties, there appears to be little chance that the treatment of Arab Jerusalem will improve. At least for the foreseeable future, "reunited" Jerusalem is likely to remain a tale of two cities.
WILLIAMSON[8]

EXAMPLE 2: CHANGING MOTIVATIONS OF ISRAELI SETTLERS IN THE OCCUPIED TERRITORIES

CONFIDENTIAL
R 201400z May 92
FM AMCONSUL JERUSALEM
TO SECSTATE WASHDC 7444
INFO AMEMBASSY AMMAN
AMEMBASSY DAMASCUS
AMEMBASSY TEL AVIV
CONFIDENTIAL JERUSALEM 01953
E.O. 12356: DECL: OADR
TAGS; PBTS, PREL, PINR, KPAL, PHUM, IS, US
SUBJECT: CHANGING MOTIVATIONS OF ISRAELI SETTLERS IN THE OCCUPIED TERRITORIES

1.   CONFIDENTIAL — ENTIRE TEXT
SUMMARY
2.   Attitudes among the 110,000 Israeli settlers in the occupied territories are hardening. Conventional wisdom over the past decade held that, following the wave of ideological settlement between 1977 and 1983, most Israelis who have moved across the green line since then were motivated primarily by economic incentives rather than by religious or nationalistic concerns. A majority of the settlers were seen more as opportunistic than political. Many settlement-watchers, however, now believe that a sizable proportion of those supposedly economic settlers have in fact become ideologues after actually living in the territories for a few years. The Intifada and the ongoing Arab-Israeli talks have polarized opinion even in commuter

settlements and have driven many previously non-political settlers into the militantly nationalistic camp.

3.   As a result, experts believe, any attempt by a future Israeli government to dismantle some settlements, limit construction, or grant meaningful autonomy to Palestinians would likely provoke fierce resistance, probably including civil disobedience, within a broad cross-section of the settler population. Some of our interlocutors speculate that as many as one-fourth of today's settlers — 27,000 people — might refuse to leave the territories even if the Israeli government ordered them to do so as part of a negotiated solution.

END SUMMARY

CONVENTIONAL WISDOM ON SETTLER MOTIVES

4.   Israelis move across the green line into settlements in the occupied West Bank and Gaza for a variety of reasons which fall into three broad categories: religious, nationalistic, and economic. Religious motivations inspire the most tenacious and uncompromising settlers. For these people, all of the land west of the Jordan (and, for some, much of the area east of the river as well) falls within the area divinely promised to the Jews in biblical times. They believe that the 1967 war and the subsequent opening of Judea, Samaria and Gaza for Jewish settlement are a fulfillment of prophecy. Settlement rabbis [names redacted] have explained to Congenoff that "resettlement" of these areas is a religious obligation that will hasten the coming of the Messiah. No contemporary argument can dissuade settlers motivated primarily by these religious dictates.

5.   Nationalistic motivations focus on Israel's need to retain the West Bank and Gaza for security in the face of hostile Arab neighbors. According to this reasoning, the pre-1967 borders are untenable, and the territories serve, at a minimum, as a much-needed buffer security zone. The presence of large numbers of Jewish civilian settlements in the occupied territories is intended to make it impossible for any Israeli government to contemplate ceding these areas to Arab sovereignty in the future. Some settler ideologues contend that the settlements themselves enhance Israeli security by holding the high ground, controlling the major arteries, and providing the Army with safe havens in the West Bank.

6.   Economic inducements in recent years have attracted many Israelis to the

occupied territories, mostly to the large commuter settlements that serve as "bedroom communities" for people who work in Tel Aviv or Jerusalem. A combination of government subsidies, tax breaks, and special mortgages have made buying a home in the territories considerably cheaper — sometimes by as much as half — than purchasing one in pre-1967 Israel. Moreover, the pleasant, suburban-style single-family houses with yards at many settlements cannot be had at any price near urban centers in Israel proper. At the same time, settlements boast a higher quality of life than crowded Israeli cities. Economically motivated settlers are drawn by the beautifully planned modern communities, tightly knit schools, clean air, and panoramic views of the surrounding countryside.

7. The conventional wisdom of most settlement-watchers over the past decade held that a majority of new Israeli inhabitants of the territories are motivated primarily by economic incentives. According to this thinking, the militantly ideological Gush Emunim movement exhausted the supply of religious and nationalistic settlers during the 1977–83 wave of settlement that followed Likud's accession to power. Since then, proponents contend, most Israelis who chose to move across the green line were not particularly ideological and were mainly seeking a cheaper home within reasonable commuting distance. A corollary of this theory was that a majority of these economically-oriented settlers would accept, more or less willingly, to move elsewhere if the GOI [government of Israel] told them to do so to fulfill a negotiated Arab-Israeli peace accord, and if the settlers were appropriately compensated.

THE POLARIZATION OF THE SETTLER POPULATION

8. Many settlement-watchers, however, now believe that a sizable proportion of those supposedly economic settlers have become ideologues after actually living in the territories for a few years. Officials of Yesha (Council of Jewish Communities in Judea, Samarra, and Gaza) and of various individual settlements have claimed to Congenoff that a clear pattern has emerged over the past decade: people move to the territories mainly for economic reasons but, within a year or two, find themselves caught up in the infectious ideology of the settlement movement. According to Yesha officials, most new settlers develop an "attachment" for the land that draws them closer to Gush Emunim.

9. Congenoff's own frequent discussions with settlers tend to confirm this trend. Random groups of residents of a wide range of settlements, polled by Congenoff over the past nine months, rarely referred to the economic advantages of living in the occupied territories, but rather spoke fervently about their biblical roots in the land and about Israel's need for the West Bank in order to survive. Predictably, strong ideological views prevail among settlers in the 50-odd Gush Emunim and 20-odd Likud-affiliated fortress communities on West Bank mountaintops. Equally unsurprisingly, inhabitants of the 20 mostly Labor-party-affiliated agricultural farms in the Jordan Valley, many of which are struggling financially, cite national security above economics as their principal motivation for remaining there.

10. Most specialists did not foresee, however, that many residents of the 20-odd burgeoning "urban" settlements within commuting distance of Jerusalem or Tel Aviv would also begin to profess a deep ideological commitment to the land. These "bedroom communities", often located just minutes from the green line, are supposed to be the home of the opportunistic, economically-motivated settlers whose decisions were based on dispassionate pragmatism. In fact, Congenoff has repeatedly heard intense nationalistic and sometimes religious arguments advanced by residents of Ma'Aleh, Adumim, Ariel, Efrat, Alfe Menashe, Qarne Shomeron, and other large settlements — which collectively contain more than half of the total settler population.

11. Two Israeli academics who have conducted extensive research into settler attitudes, [names redacted], separately confirmed to Congenoff that this polarization process is occurring. [Name redacted] asserted that no Israeli moves across the green line without a keen awareness of the political and practical significance of doing so; therefore, even settlers initially attracted by cheaper homes felt no ideological qualms about living in the occupied territories. At a minimum, according to [name redacted], economic settlers start out "neutral" on the issue in principle. Once they are firmly ensconced in a settlement, however, these settlers are "seduced" by the religious and nationalistic arguments that justify their controversial decision. [Name redacted] sees a clear rightward shift in the thinking of the large "commuter" population in settlements.

12. [Two lines redacted] pointed out that Israelis generally are more ideological

than most other nationalities, and therefore few economic settlers remain uncommitted in the highly charged, ideological environment of the West Bank and Gaza. [Name redacted] stressed that most settlers have overlapping motivations, and that many of those who first crossed the green line in search of a better mortgage deal were probably latent ideologues. In [name redacted]'s view, it is a mistake to "label" any settler as purely economically motivated. He perceives growing support throughout the settler community for Likud hard-liners and political parties further to the right.

13. Both [names redacted] are convinced that the Intifada has also driven many previously non-political settlers into the militantly nationalistic camp. Being shot at and stoned on a daily basis, noted [name redacted], prompted settlement residents to "circle the wagons" and to harden their opinions of the Palestinians. For many settlers, the Intifada proved that it would be dangerous for Israel ever to allow the territories to revert to Arab sovereignty; it reinforced in them a sense of purpose about their presence there. The current peace negotiations, which raised the specter of the settlers' worst nightmare — "territorial compromise" — have had a similar effect. Even Yesha officials have confided to Congenoff that the Intifada and the Madrid conference injected new life into the ideological settlement movement.

IMPLICATIONS

14. This gradual polarization of settler attitudes increases the likelihood that the settlement population, which could double to 220,000 over the next five years if the building boom continues, will in itself be an intractable obstacle to any negotiated arrangement for the territories. Ideological settlers bitterly oppose any restrictions on their activities, and vehemently denounce Palestinian autonomy as a perilous trap. Any hypothetical attempt by a future Israeli government to dismantle some settlements, limit construction, or grant meaningful autonomy to Palestinians would likely provoke fierce resistance throughout the settler population. [Name redacted] predicts that the front line of such resistance would be widespread civil disobedience, possibly including blocking roads, refusing to pay taxes, staging mass demonstrations, and, perhaps most importantly, proceeding with unauthorized new settlement construction.

15. Beyond civil disobedience, [name redacted] sees a very real potential
    among settler ideologues for acts of armed resistance to the peace process.
    While observers remain unanimous that settler leaders will seek to avoid
    any clash with the Army (which remains a sacrosanct institution for them),
    there is nonetheless growing concern over what [name redacted] calls
    "provocative terrorism" against Arabs. A handful of settler extremists, for
    example, could spark a violent Palestinian reaction by blowing up a
    mosque or assassinating a Palestinian leader. [Name redacted] warns that
    many Gush Emunim zealots are experienced in military commando
    operations and explosives.

16. The polarization of the settler community raises the following question,
    with which [several words redacted] settlement-watchers are wrestling: if a
    future Israeli government ever tried to dismantle certain West Bank
    settlements as part of a negotiated solution, as it did in the Sinai, how
    many settlers would dig in and refuse to leave their homes? Although our
    interlocutors say that much would depend on the circumstances (such as
    whether the government in power was Likud or Labor), they speculate that
    as many as one-fourth of today's settlers — 27,000 people — might defy
    government orders. [Approximately four lines redacted.]

17. While it is difficult to predict behavior shifts in the face of a real prospect
    for peace, this polarization is increasingly evident. Moreover, settlers say
    they learned a lesson from the withdrawal from Sinai. During those
    negotiations, they accepted GOI advice to hold their fire until agreement
    was reached. This time, settlers claim — and many Israeli analysts caution
    — settlers will make their objections clear from the outset to preempt any
    GOI negotiating position that could preclude their future in the occupied
    territories.

    WILLIAMSON[9]

It is not difficult to see why these reports would have been singled out. First, they
deal with two of the key issues that will have to be resolved in any lasting peace agreement between Israel and its neighbors: the status of Jerusalem and the status of settlements on the West Bank. These are politically charged issues that the author of the
reports treats with dispassion and clarity, citing an impressive array of sources to buttress
two fundamental conclusions, both of which challenged conventional wisdom: (1) that

Jerusalem, far from being the model of peaceful existence between Arabs and Jews that Israeli leaders contended, was a segregated city in which few resources had been devoted either to promoting a common space or to providing municipal services for the Arab inhabitants; (2) that West Bank settlers of more recent origins would be less ideologically motivated than their predecessors and therefore more persuadable about giving up their property for a financial settlement in the context of an overall peace agreement. In nominating Steven Kashkett for the award, the consul general said in part:

> [His] political reporting is the finest I've had occasion to witness in my almost two decades in the Foreign Service. His portfolio includes two of the most volatile issues in the Middle East: Israeli settlement in the occupied territories and the politics of Jerusalem. These two issues surfaced at the outset of our peace efforts and continued to plague the process without respite. Our delicate orchestration relied heavily on the clear, thoroughly-researched and balanced presentations Mr. Kashkett has provided Washington decision-makers, as they have repeatedly acknowledged to me.[10]

In his personal assessment of the merits of the reports, Kashkett cited two elements:

> First, they shed light on aspects of the situation in Jerusalem and the West Bank that were not well understood but were nonetheless vital to policymakers. Second, both of these cables combined factual reporting with candid, no-holds-barred analysis throughout.[11]

Of the six criteria cited by awards committees for their decisions, the consul general's nomination explicitly mentions the top three: usefulness, analytical and interpretive content, and sources and contacts. Two others—cultural and linguistic skills and groundbreaking content—are clearly implicit in the language of the nomination. The only criterion that does not emerge clearly in the materials available is style, although that appears to have been simply an omission. The reports are clear, readable, and well organized. The style enhances the content, rather than obscuring it.

CHAPTER EIGHT

CASE STUDY I: THE COLLAPSE OF THE SOVIET UNION:
Early Embassy Moscow Views

This chapter is a case study of diplomatic political analysis, using as examples two cables submitted by Embassy Moscow. The first is from July 1990, when the embassy initially suggested that the Soviet Union might collapse. The second was submitted in December 1990, as the process of disintegration accelerated. The following chapter also concerns the collapse of the Soviet Union but is a case study of embassy reporting during a period of intense crisis: the August 1991 coup intended to end political and economic reform. The failure of that coup marked the death of the Soviet Union, although it was not formally taken off life support for another four months. The four cables are snapshots of how the embassy attempted to carry out its analytical and advisory functions during this fast-moving and momentous period.

A few disclaimers are in order. Obviously, these particular reports were not chosen at random. Some of the reasons for choosing them were entirely practical. Since I drafted them, I know the circumstances and thought processes that produced them in a way that no one else can. There is always the danger that 20/20 hindsight and the fact that they are examples of my own craftsmanship may interfere with my ability to evaluate them, and the reader should keep that in mind. I am mindful of the fact that the cables were either somewhat prescient or marked an historic moment. If that had not been the case, I might not have kept the titles, dates, and cable numbers in my personal records. Having this information at hand made it far more practical for me to request the department to go through the formal process of declassifying (or declining to declassify) the cables. Since most embassy analytical efforts are classified, using any of them as case studies in a book like this requires prior declassification. As I have previously indicated, the State Department made it impossible or impractical for me to seek declassification of reports that had been nominated for awards. Thus, with the exception of the two cables presented in the previous chapter, I was left with no recourse except to fall back upon my own drafting efforts. Aside from the value indicated above of using my own work, it does seem appropriate for an author who presumes to write on the subject of diplomatic political analysis to submit at least some of his own work to the readers' purview.

The reader should also be aware that I was not the original drafter on most embassy political cables during my time there. Each political counselor has to define his job in the way that seems best to him. There were about thirty people in Embassy Moscow's political section from 1988 to 1991, most of them hardworking, ambitious, and talented drafting officers. At the time, it was the largest U.S. embassy political section in the world. Although I prefer writing my own material to editing that of others, I made a conscious decision that I could add the most value to embassy reporting as a whole by providing ideas and direction to my staff, polishing and editing their work, and not letting it languish unread on my desk. My own earlier experience had convinced me that nothing erodes the morale of a political analyst more than having his work sit on the desk of his superior unread and untransmitted for days or weeks. My rule was either to act on a draft within twenty-four hours or tell the drafting officer why I needed more time. I spent many Saturday hours working on drafts that required more of my time than I could spare during the Monday to Friday period. Interestingly, a recipient of the director general's reporting award cited as one of the chief obstacles to effective Embassy reporting "supervisors . . . who either slowed down the reporting process while agonizing over the difference between 'happy' and 'glad' or those who didn't recognize important issues that lay just over the horizon."[1] Another recipient noted the important role of the reviewing officer: "Every one of my best cables benefited from the consul general's comments. I often knew a cable would be good because it was so difficult to get past the CG. For that to work, the reviewer needs to have the knowledge and be willing to spend the time to think along with the drafter. I actually think most bad cables are the fault of the reviewing officer."[2]

When I drafted cables, it was generally for one of two reasons. Either I believed that I had a perspective on an issue that I could only communicate adequately by drafting it myself, or external circumstances required me to shortcut the usual drafting and clearing process. The first two cables below are examples of the former situation. During the coup against Soviet president Gorbachev in August 1991, both situations existed. I did most of the embassy's analytical reporting during that period because events were moving so quickly and because, after three years on the job and two decades of background, I thought that I was best equipped to interpret developments, understand their meaning, and communicate it quickly to Washington.

With those disclaimers and caveats in mind, let us look at the cables below in light of previous chapters on the craft of political analysis.

LOOKING INTO THE ABYSS: THE POSSIBLE COLLAPSE OF THE SOVIET UNION, AND WHAT WE SHOULD BE DOING ABOUT IT

In July 1990, some eighteen months before it happened, I drafted, and the embassy approved and submitted, a cable that posited a possible collapse of the Soviet Union and made a number of recommendations for policies that could protect and advance U.S. interests if such a collapse should occur. The text of that cable, declassified by the State Department at my request, is reproduced on the following pages:

SECRET

O 131042Z JUL 90

FM AMEMBASSY MOSCOW

TO SECSTATE WASHDC IMMEDIATE 6647

INFO MOSCOW POLITICAL COLLECTIVE

AMCONSUL LENINGRAD

SECRET MOSCOW 23603

EXDIS

E.O. 12356: DECL:OADR

TAGS: PREL, PINT, ECON, EFIN, UR, US

SUJBECT: LOOKING INTO THE ABYSS: THE POSSIBLE COLLAPSE OF THE SOVIET UNION AND WHAT WE SHOULD BE DOING ABOUT IT

1. Secret — Entire Text.

SUMMARY

2. Gorbachev, or even more progressive reformers, may triumph and the Soviet Union may move rapidly into full and productive interaction with the rest of the world. But they also may not, and it appears to us that the potentially less happy outcomes are the ones that require more

forethought. The prospects of the Gorbachev regime have deteriorated over the past year and Soviets themselves are increasingly talking in apocalyptic terms. Some Republics will leave the Soviet Union and there will be a substantial redefinition of the remaining Republics' relationship to the center and to each other unless massive repression is used to prevent it. Truly dangerous scenarios — ranging from civil war and the loss of control over nuclear weapons to a truncated, belligerent, nuclear-armed Soviet or Russian state — cannot be excluded, even if they are not as likely as less apocalyptic scenarios. We need to take a close look at our policy to make certain that it minimizes the probability of extreme outcomes, and minimizes the risks to the U.S. if they should occur despite our best efforts.

3.   We should move now to establish a permanent presence in each of the Soviet Republics. A major expansion of our exchange programs, both governmental and private, is essential. We need to keep our focus, and that of the Gorbachev regime, on moving forward on economic reform. Our arms control negotiations are in serious danger of being a day late and a dollar short. We need to rethink our objectives and how we are going to get there, from war-fighting strategy to modernization to how we organize ourselves as a government to conduct arms control negotiations. We need to move beyond ad hoc-isms in civil conflicts to the establishment of international principles and mechanisms for dealing with them.   END SUMMARY.

DOMESTIC SITUATION: NO BOTTOM YET IN SIGHT

4.   "We are looking into the abyss," says a young Soviet we've met a couple of times, an interpreter at the Foreign Ministry. Clenching his fists, he continues, "I'm so frustrated, because there is nothing I can do about this situation." Then, with a defeated shrug of his shoulders he adds, "Nothing much can be expected of my generation anyway. We're all cynics. We were raised under Brezhnev."

5.   This was not an isolated remark. The most common phrase we hear in our discussions these days with Soviets is "I am afraid. I do not know what is going to happen." When a Russian looks into the abyss, he sees horrors of which, happily, Americans are only dimly aware. For every American soldier killed in World War II, some 90 Soviet men, women and children died. We had a short period of McCarthyism, while the Soviets were killing perhaps 20 million of their own people under Stalin. We experienced the

depression and the dustbowl; the Soviets collectivization, deportation and mass starvation.

6. Perhaps this ever-present sense of standing on the brink of catastrophe accounts for the perpetual nervosity of the Moscow intelligentsia, its continual conviction that a conservative coup is looming. Yet an outside observer's evaluation can be only somewhat more reassuring. The economic situation continues to deteriorate, with no bottom yet in sight. Economic regionalism and autarky grow daily, casting doubt on the continued ability of the national economy to function as a system, and even raising questions about the central government's ability to get food and other basics to the major urban areas. At the same time, processes are under way which if successful over the longer-term will modernize this still archaic society; primary among them are a significant decentralization of economic and political power and a nearly complete end to conscious isolationism and national autarky.

7. The political unity of the country is dissolving. A Soviet historian recently told us he hopes that in 30-50 years natural forces will bring some of the Soviet Republics back together. Meanwhile, he hopes that the Soviet Union can remain, not a superpower, but at least a great power, one of the 10 major world powers. If the Ukraine and Byelorussia separate, he says, even that will not be possible. Russia might be reduced to the borders of Muscovy. Clearly, even if a process of dissolution does not go that far, the political relationships within and among the constituent Republics are bound to be redefined considerably. They will continue to have shared economic interests, especially because of the present highly interdependent industrial infrastructure.

8. The structure of Soviet post-war security has collapsed. The military is being asked to take large budget cuts at the same time that the Soviet Union's primary military alliance has effectively ceased to function and its geographic barrier to invasion is disappearing. Negotiations or unilateral reductions are eliminating, and sometimes reversing, former Soviet numerical advantages in personnel and several categories of weaponry.

ALTERNATIVE FUTURES

9. The Gorbachev regime may survive, muddle through, and even eventually triumph over this sea of troubles. Moreover, a regime pressing for even

more rapid and thorough reform could replace Gorbachev's. Nevertheless, the risk of retrograde movement, of increasing disorder, even of anarchy is greater now than it was in the past. This raises the question of whether any adjustments should be made in US policy to limit downside risks. The issue is not whether a happier outcome is more probable. We do not exclude the possibility that the progressives may triumph and that the Soviet Union may move rapidly into full and productive interaction with the rest of the world. It is simply that happier outcomes demand less forethought.

10. If Gorbachev is able to remain in power and, even with many zigs and zags, move a reform program forward, we will be dealing in the near future with a Soviet Union that is very different from today's. The Baltics will break away and form independent states. Georgia and Moldova may do likewise. Political independence may go further than true economic sovereignty in these areas, given natural trade relations and the highly linked, dependent nature of the Soviet economy. Economic and ethnic realities appear to make independence a less likely option for the other Soviet Republics, but with feelings of nationalism exploding in the country today we should not assume that a rational calculation of economic and political costs and benefits will prevail. At a minimum, the remaining Soviet Union will contain republics with a variety of ties to the center, some probably quite loose. Growing resistance to serving in the Soviet army will probably require the establishment of something akin to national guards in the remaining Republics. The Red Army will face increasing pressure to become a professional force, although not necessarily an all-Russian one.

11. Worse scenarios are possible. Perhaps the most dangerous would be civil war, accompanied by the division of the Soviet Union into multiple independent states of varying degrees of viability, some possessing nuclear weapons and delivery systems. Only slightly less dangerous would be the breakup of the Soviet Union and the reversion of Russia into an authoritarian, autarkic system, hostile to an outside world that it saw as exploitative in its time of weakness and possessing the Soviet nuclear arsenal. A somewhat less dangerous alternative, though hardly one we would desire, is fulfillment of the Moscow intelligentsia's fears of a conservative coup — the establishment of an authoritarian regime that

would repress breakaway nationalist movements and repress dissent. It is doubtful that such a regime would move overtly and militarily against its erstwhile Eastern European allies, but it would covet them and could be expected to maneuver to bring them back into its orbit.

US POLICY: PRINCIPLES

12. How can we hedge US policy against the more negative of these outcomes? What, if anything, can we do to make them less probable? A few basic principles should guide our policy. It is particularly important now that we not confuse the pursuit of short-term advantage with the advancement of basic interests. We need to avoid superimposing US/Soviet tensions on Soviet internal problems. And we should be pursuing a web of relationships that minimizes the danger of an autarkic, belligerent shift and limits its duration and intensity, if it should occur.

US POLICY: PRACTICE

13. How do these principles translate into a foreign policy program? First of all, a basic US interest continues to be the opening of Soviet society. It has become more important than ever, in fact we believe it has become a significant interest of the United States, to have a physical presence in each of the Soviet republics and in a number of additional locations in Russia. It is increasingly evident as these regions evolve toward greater independence that our ties with them should not be funneled through Moscow. This embassy has for about 18 months been urging the establishment of small posts in a number of Soviet cities, thus far to no avail. We will in a subsequent table be setting out some further ideas about how this might be accomplished now, while discussions about the eventual size and configuration of such posts continue.

14. Establishing a multiplicity of ties with different regions and elements of Soviet society also requires a dramatic expansion of our USIA programs here, particularly the IV program, and of opportunities for training in business management. We should encourage a major expansion of programs, most of which might be private, to bring young Soviets to the US for year-long periods of study. We believe we could do more to promote US interests and Western values in this country with $2 million in exchanges than with $2 billion in consumer goods, unless the larger sum was tightly linked to badly needed and politically sensitive economic policy changes.

We should look into whether there might be an appropriate role for the Peace Corps here. Such a presence would contribute to the immediate opening of Soviet society. It would also offer the possibility of dramatically expanded contacts with today's young Soviet professionals. These are the people who, if the current leadership generation's push for reform exhausts itself, are likely to lead the country's next major reform effort.

15. Our military-to-military ties are becoming even more important. They represent a link to one of the most crucial all-union organizations and can work to influence its transition to an institution more inclined to seek a harmonious process of decentralization than to intervene to prevent it. Such contacts can also prevent a dangerous sense of isolation from developing among Soviet military and civilian strategists who see their postwar security structure crumbling.

16. We consider it improbable that any likely successor regime or leader would have as enlightened a view of Soviet foreign policy interests as Gorbachev. Moreover, he may represent the best hope for a relatively stable, and therefore less dangerous transition to a new type of society and a new set of relationships among the Republics. Nevertheless, we should avoid the temptation to undertake economic aid simply to subsidize Gorbachev's regime. This is not a poor country. It has enormous resources and an educated (albeit badly trained and almost totally unmotivated) population. Its system and its practices squander those resources on a huge scale. We should not help a Soviet regime avoid the hard choices that in the longer run will be beneficial to the Soviet Union and make it a more suitable international partner. On the other hand, anything we can do to help them make those hard choices and follow through on them, we should do. The President's initiative at the Houston Summit on the question of assistance to the Soviet Union represents a major step toward finding a multilateral approach to dealing with the fundamental problems of the Soviet economy. An IMF/IBRD led effort will be crucial for all parties. Our comments on improving US technical assistance will be addressed in a separate cable.

17. We are far behind the curve, perhaps dangerously so, in arms control negotiations. We should at this point be implementing START and CFE and be well along in negotiations on START II and CFE II. Under any scenario we can think of, a Soviet Union with 2500 deliverable nuclear weapons has

got to be less dangerous than one with 12,000. It is clear to everyone that one of the chief problems in Europe today is the lag of military reductions and adjustments behind political developments. The issue here is what we can do on our side, or perhaps in agreement with the Soviets, to get out of the bureaucratic thickets on arms control negotiations and move forward more aggressively. Would it be possible, for example, to create a senior, blue-ribbon group outside of the arms control negotiations process, and also outside of the interagency process, but with access to the issues each has under consideration, to identify hangups and recommend solutions to US leaders at the cabinet level and in the White House? We should take the lead in capping the arms race by limiting modernization. This would allow us to lock in areas of US qualitative superiority, although we should avoid the temptation to press for modernization limits only in those areas. The embassy now believes that the more important nuclear threat we face is not that the Soviet government will use nuclear arms against us, but rather that control over those arms might slip out of its hands. We should focus more of our arms control attention on limiting or eliminating those systems of mass destruction that are most likely to fall into unstable hands. ICBMs may be much less a threat to us or other nations someday than tactical and local nuclear devices that may be used, stolen or sold to third parties under worst-case Soviet disintegration scenarios.

18. On regional conflicts, we should move aggressively to challenge the Soviets to adopt a different approach to dealing with civil conflicts in the Third World. Together, by agreeing not to supply arms in such conflicts and to establish international mediation efforts, we could end many of them, limit the destructiveness of others, and keep them from becoming dangerous in the bilateral context. This is already the direction our policy is going in practice. We should formalize it in some way, perhaps by a suitable joint resolution in the UN.

19. In many respects, as the recommendations above indicate, our policy is already on the right track. We may only need to do more, or to do it faster. But in some areas we need to change conceptual frameworks that have become comfortable over recent decades. The dramatic cuts in weapons of mass destruction that are now possible, for example, cuts that could do much to limit the dangers of a retrogressive turn in Soviet society or policy, will

require a major rethinking of our military strategy and objectives. We face a period of unique opportunities, but also potentially one of unique dangers. It is a time that calls for prudence, but not timidity. A failsafe policy in dealing with the turmoil in Soviet society will surely fail, but it will not be safe. It will cause us to miss the opportunities, while adding to the dangers.

MATLOCK[3]

Why This Subject, at This Time?

In late June 1990, the Foreign Ministry invited the U.S. Embassy to take part in a foreign policy conference that it was sponsoring. The conference included Soviet and American historians, as well as Foreign Ministry officials. Normally, I would have given one of the officers in my section the opportunity to attend the conference rather than being out of the office for a couple of days myself. In this case, something about the conference—I no longer remember what—piqued my interest, and I decided to attend. The most valuable part of the conference, as is often the case, turned out to be the opportunity to talk informally with the attendees during breaks and meals. Something—perhaps the setting, perhaps the subject matter—led to an unusual degree of openness during my conversations with the Soviet historians and Foreign Ministry officials present, which included the exchanges with the interpreter and historian cited in paragraphs four and seven of the cable.

As I listened, particularly to the historian's depiction of the truncated Soviet Union he foresaw, I recognized that I was hearing something important. If he thought this way, he could not be alone. If thoughtful, educated Soviet citizens were contemplating the collapse of the Soviet Union, why were we not? I started my notes for the cable that evening and began drafting it as soon as I returned to the embassy.

Analysis, Prediction, and Policy Recommendations

The purpose of this cable was not to predict the imminent breakup of the Soviet Union. In fact, the cable explicitly mentioned other possible outcomes from the forces then at work in Soviet society. Occasionally, intelligence agencies may have reliable information about an event that is about to occur. At that point, however, informing policymakers is not prediction, but simply factual reporting. In political affairs, with its myriad of unknown or unquantifiable factors, prediction is essentially an exercise in probability analysis. It requires filtering the most accurate information available through the mind of an informed analyst, who adds a soupçon of judgment or of art and makes his best guess. If he is modest, he qualifies it appropriately. Many political leaders abhor ambiguity. They have to make decisions based on inevitably limited information and want more help in making those decisions than is provided by an analysis that offers them no practical alternatives. The challenge is to provide analysis that conveys the complexity of a situation without getting so wrapped up in the complexity as to be meaningless as an input to decision making.

Putting the words "the possible collapse of the Soviet Union" in the title of this embassy cable was, in the context of the times, a deliberately dramatic step intended to draw attention to the analysis that followed. Its primary objective was encompassed in the subsequent "what we should be doing about it," which recommended both policies and specific steps that would protect U.S. interests in the event of a collapse. In making specific policy recommendations, the embassy sought an audience for this cable that included officials higher than the desk officers and intelligence community analysts who would be the normal audience for strictly analytical efforts. We used both an attention-getting phrase in the title and a technical means of restricting the audience for the cable as a way of aiming for that higher audience. (Chapter 3's "Targeting Your Audience" section discusses the paradox of restricting cable distribution as a way of getting higher-level attention.)

It seems fair to conclude that the cable did reach the intended audience. During a visit to Moscow, then president George H. W. Bush told me that he saw some of the embassy's reporting—not much, but some. The "abyss cable" seems to have been one of the cables he saw. We indicated in chapter 3 that it is extremely rare for a president to read an embassy cable. They do not have time. What they have in abundance is talented people filtering and digesting masses of material, deciding what warrants their time and attention. However, in the 1990 context, a cable with the words "the possible collapse of the Soviet Union" in the title might have been sufficiently unusual to have passed through the filters. Subsequent to transmission of the embassy's abyss cable, in the summer of 1990, the Washington intelligence community was asked to assess the likelihood of the collapse of the Soviet Union. It concluded "not likely," although it had considered the abyss cable of sufficient interest to include in its top secret briefing to ambassadors at key embassies.[4]

Principles of Post-Containment Policy: The Embassy's Road Not Taken

The recommendations in Embassy Moscow's abyss cable involved both general principles and concrete actions in specific areas. The underlying principle can be simply stated:

U.S. interests would be better served by drawing the Soviet state into a productive web of relationships with the West, thereby reinforcing reformist tendencies, than by exploiting any disarray for short-term advantage. The latter policy risked superimposing U.S.-Soviet tensions on Soviet domestic problems and reinforcing the autarkic tendencies that represent one of the deep-rooted elements of Russian political culture. It is clear that these principles did not become the basis for post-containment policy, which emphasized expanding NATO eastward rather than drawing Russia into the Western economic system.

A Balance Sheet on the Specific Recommendations

The specific steps were intended to support reform and to mitigate the risk of worst-case scenarios. They included:

- Expanding ties to the non-Russian Soviet republics
- Deepening understanding of Western, particularly American, culture and business practices
- Targeting assistance programs to support reform
- Speeding up arms control efforts
- Seeking greater cooperation and less competition in dealing with Third World conflicts[5]

Since I was in Moscow until September 1991, I can in large part only speculate on the impact this embassy dispatch and its recommendations had in Washington. If nothing happened, it seems only fair to conclude that an embassy recommendation had little or no impact. On the other hand, if something happened, it might indicate that the embassy recommendation was decisive, or that it simply supported decisions largely already approved. With that in mind, here are some impressions.

The arms control process was broken in 1990. Strategic arms reduction negotiations had been going on for nine years and were mired in technical and verification minutiae that could be, and were, used by hostile elements in both countries to delay agreement. U.S. and Soviet leaders did re-engage through the talks in fall 1990 and reported some progress. The START I agreement was finally ready for signature during President Bush's July 1991 visit to Moscow, weeks before the August coup against Gorbachev. The collapse of that coup effectively ended central control in the USSR. The formal dissolution of the Soviet Union in December 1991 created a danger that the embassy had foreseen: several republics emerged from the dissolution with nuclear weapons and delivery systems. Fortunately, Russia and the United States made quick and, although there were some initial difficulties, ultimately effective progress, convincing these new states that their interests would not be served by becoming nuclear powers. They promptly agreed to transfer the weapons and delivery systems to Russia. The Departments of Defense, State, and Energy subsequently set up assistance programs to provide better security in the former Soviet Union for fissile materials and to decrease the likelihood they could be smuggled across borders, another danger cited in the embassy's cable. Congress initiated this process with passage of the 1991 Nunn-Lugar legislation, which established program authority and funding to assist in securing the vast stockpiles of Soviet weapons of mass destruction and related materials.

The two countries took some steps to limit their rivalry in the Third World, including jointly sponsoring a Middle East resolution in the UN rather than tabling separate, mutually incompatible resolutions. They cooperated productively in attempting to put an end to conflicts in Angola, Nicaragua, El Salvador, and Cambodia.

The United States expanded its student exchange and International Visitor programs somewhat, although far less than the embassy considered desirable. It consistently sought to align its bilateral aid efforts with economic reform—a delicate area, as the line between helpful assistance and unacceptable interference is murky. Happily, however, it encouraged the World Bank and International Monetary Fund to take the lead in this area. It was clear that even under optimum conditions economic reform would, in the short run, entail further pain for the Soviet people, which would lead to blame and disillusionment. International institutions belonged at the center of this effort, not the United States.

This cable renewed the ambassador's 1989 recommendation to establish offices in certain of the Soviet republics. The earlier recommendation had been accepted in principle but, essentially, pocket-vetoed because no resources had been allocated to make it happen.[6] After the cable, the State Department made concrete plans to open several such offices and put people into language training to staff them. As a result, when Secretary James Baker in early 1992 ordered that embassies be established immediately in each of the newly independent states, there actually existed a small, though still woefully inadequate, cadre of partially trained personnel to build the new embassies around.

Given enough time, the governmental bureaucracy can shift resources and generate new policies to meet changed opportunities or challenges. However, it would have taken decisive, perhaps even visionary, leadership at the highest levels for the United States to respond adequately to the speed and depth of change occurring in Soviet society. On the other hand, perhaps it is fairer to say that the United States did respond "adequately" to this challenge. A world-spanning ideology imploded, a massive military alliance broke up, and the largest country/empire in the world collapsed over a breathtakingly brief period of time without a war and with little loss of life. If most of the credit for that belongs to the people and leaders of the countries directly involved, perhaps it is also fair to say that U.S. policies played a constructive, rather than detrimental, role in those processes and that embassy reporting during the period contributed to those policies.

Elements of the Craft (1)

Although I am far from a brilliant linguist, I had sufficient capability in Russian to engage in meaningful conversations with my interlocutors. My political and cultural background allowed me to recognize something important when I heard it. I made the conceptual leap from dismissing a development as so improbable as not to be worth considering, to possible. Having made that leap, I put the possibility into the larger context of how it might affect my country's interests. I made an effort to reach an audience appropriate for what I had to say. I attempted to communicate in a succinct, straightforward, although hopefully not pedestrian, writing style. The cable was sufficiently explicit and detailed in its policy recommendations that it risked being seen in Washington as critical of how the White House and State Department were handling U.S.-Soviet relations. While that perception would not have been far from the mark (at least on some issues), it would not have produced an outlook at the policy level conducive to actually moving forward on the recommendations. Therefore, I made every effort to couch them in terms that were neutral or, indeed, flattering to policymakers by putting them in the context of the administration's overall policy approach.

POWER, AUTHORITY, AND LEGITIMACY IN THE USSR

By December 1990, five months later, Gorbachev had engaged in a series of tacks back and forth between the conservative and reformist positions—tacks that he, no doubt, saw as tactical maneuvers but that created the impression of a system veering out of control. In late summer, he appeared to be supporting a far-reaching economic reform plan that economic officers at the embassy believed could be effective. Subsequently, following reports of movements by military units outside of Moscow, Gorbachev backed away from key elements of that plan. Whether the troop movements actually occurred or were tied to Gorbachev's veer away from reform has never been clarified, but I have always considered the timing of the two events significant. The apparent ascendancy of anti-reform elements in the Soviet hierarchy occurred as independence movements in some Soviet republics, autonomy movements in others, were growing. I tried to tie these developments to more fundamental processes in the following cable:

SECRET
O 121305Z DEC90
FM AMEMBASSY MOSCOW
TO SECSTATE WASHDC IMMEDIATE 8014
INFO RUEHXD/MOSCOW POLITICAL COLLECTIVE
AMCONSUL LENINGRAD
SECRET MOSCOW 43102
EXDIS
E.O. 12356: DECL:OADR
TAGS: PREL, PGOV, PINR, ECON, UR
SUBJECT: POWER, AUTHORITY AND LEGITIMACY IN THE USSR
TODAY
REF: (A) MOSCOW 41464; (B) MOSCOW 42121

1.   Secret — Entire Text.
2.   SUMMARY: The paralysis of authority in Soviet society today results from
     the failure of economic reform, a collapse of unifying values, an absence of
     legitimacy at the top and an unwillingness to use force. Gorbachev has
     been unable to articulate a new set of values sufficiently accepted to
     provide a basis on which to build his reformed Soviet Union. Instead, and
     in the absence of any economic payoff from over five years of *perestroyka*,
     public enthusiasm has been evoked only by ethnic nationalism and the
     ephemeral personal popularity of a few individuals. Standing against these
     accelerating centrifugal forces are some economic factors and the military
     and security apparatus, which has become a vital component of
     Gorbachev's shrinking support base. His increased reliance on the military
     and security apparatus is occurring despite personal reluctance and a
     realization that the step may be dangerous, both intrinsically and for the
     reform process. This may be Gorbachev's last chance to reassert his and the
     center's authority and re-establish sufficient stability by political means to

permit his vision of an orderly reform process to move forward. The danger for Gorbachev is that this will depend greatly on the actions of others, including political rivals such as Yeltsin. The danger for all advocates of reform is first that the initiative could pass into the hands of those who would use force, either to preserve the Union or to sunder it, and second that active economic reform may be a necessary pre-condition for stability, rather than something to be attempted after stability is assured. END SUMMARY.

3. In the intense power struggle now underway in the Soviet Union, the use of force has become extremely risky, authority has been fragmented, and legitimacy has been replaced with an ephemeral popularity. Prior to Gorbachev, the Soviet system worked because those in authority possessed power and the demonstrated willingness to use it regardless of personal popularity. A veneer of legitimacy overlay the system, comprised in part of real or imagined achievements — defeat of the Nazis, economic advancement, leadership of the worldwide Communist movement — and in part of a traditional Russian willingness to accept the right to rule of those in command. In dismantling what he calls the "command and administrative" system, Gorbachev is seeking a transition to a system in which authority is based on legitimacy, with the use of power only at the margins.

LEGITIMACY VERSUS POPULARITY

4. It is already evident that in beginning this process Gorbachev dangerously underestimated the forces that would be released when decades of repression were released. But perhaps his greatest miscalculation was in believing that the reforms he put into motion would in and of themselves convey a legitimacy on his regime that would aid it in the process of social renewal. Instead, what he received was substantial, but fragile and evanescent popularity that has been dissipated in more than five years of deepening economic crisis and inconclusive struggle with both the institutional and intellectual legacies of the past. This was accompanied by a collapse of the value system on which the old system was based. Into the moral vacuum thus created has come, not the values of a humane, democratic socialism that Gorbachev no doubt intended, but instead ethnic nationalism, personal popularity, and even more corruption propelled by economic deficits and the lifting of the fear factor.

5.   One of the most fundamental political facts in Soviet life today is the profound disgust of the great bulk of the population for all manifestations of the old power structure. Those who are seen as courageous opponents of that structure are popular. Thus, Gorbachev, the USSR Congress of People's Deputies, the USSR Supreme Soviet, Yeltsin, Gdlyan, Ivanov, the RSFSR Supreme Soviet and Kalugin have all had their moments of popular acclaim. For some that popular acclaim continues as they ride the outer edge of the politically acceptable. For others, the confrontation with hard choices has forced compromises, and with them has come a loss in public favor. Moscow's Mayor Popov, for example, has recently won a damaging fight with the City Council over its desire to fire the city's police chief (Ref A).

THE FRAGMENTATION OF AUTHORITY

6.   The "war of laws" under way between the center and the Republics, and between some of them and even smaller entities, is one of the most debilitating manifestations of the fragmentation of authority that characterizes Soviet society today. From a situation in which the possession of authority conveyed with it an almost automatic presumption of legitimacy, the Soviet Union has reached a situation today in which the ability to make authoritative decisions is challenged at every level. The result, in recent months, has been a virtual paralysis on both the political and economic fronts. A multiplicity of actors can block the implementation of policy, but none is capable of executing it. Gorbachev's decrees are ignored, which leads him to be viewed with contempt and further decreases his authority. But despite all of their sovereignty resolutions and declarations of independence the Republics have been no more capable than the center of putting real content into their declarations.

POWER

7.   Ultimate power rests, as it always has, with those controlling the instruments of violence. While the erosion of party rule may have loosened political control over the military and the KGB, the risks of using force to advance their interests may paradoxically be greater than ever. The groundswell of public revulsion against the old political structure has made any move that could be interpreted as attempting to preserve or reinstate its power and privileges dangerous for those ordering it. The dangers arise first, from the possibility of mass resistance, à la Romania; and second,

from refusal by junior officers and enlisted personnel to carry out orders.
WHO CONTROLS WHOM?

8. Gorbachev's current veer to the right (ref B) is yet another, and perhaps the last, attempt to reassert his and the center's authority by political means. In making this attempt Gorbachev is relying more heavily than ever before on the institutions whose traditions of respect for political authority have been least damaged by the country's social ferment. These institutions happen also to be the repositories of ultimate power in the system — the military, the KGB and to some extent the MVD. At the same time, Gorbachev is employing the instruments of economic and financial pressure and persuasion he has under his control to pull the Republics back from decisions that he says would amount to dissolution of the union and might result in civil war. The use of these levers requires retaining centralized control of some of the same instruments of economic activity that would devolve to the Republics or go into private hands under the more promising economic reform plans.

9. Gorbachev no doubt views his current retrenchment as a tactical maneuver, reflecting a need to re-establish sufficient authority and discipline to permit an orderly reform process to move forward. But there are two problems created by his steps. First, if Gorbachev puts key economic reform measures on hold pending achievement of stability through administrative measures, the result may be continued economic decline, leading to further instability. Second, it is not clear at this point whether the institutions and instruments on which he is now relying will prove to be his tools, or whether he will become their captive. The danger is that this will depend a great deal on the responses of others to the measures he is undertaking. If these measures produce a cycle of violent action and reaction, as they well might, the influence of those who can employ force will grow still further, and Gorbachev's authority and his room for maneuver will be still further constrained. Nothing in his record thus far indicates that Gorbachev would sanction the large-scale use of force, either to stay in office or to achieve his political goals. But there is a growing danger that the initiative could pass into the hands of those who would. This time, the crucial hour for *perestroyka* may really have come.

COLLINS[7]

In one sense, this is a more typical embassy analytical effort than the abyss cable, since it contains no explicit policy or action recommendations. In another sense, it is a bit atypical in that it is not tied to a specific development, event, or piece of new information. Read in conjunction with the abyss cable, it reinforces the sense that this is a country and a political system in crisis. Institutions are unraveling and lack a sense of legitimacy. The instruments of power are in the hands of those most opposed to the kinds of reforms that appear to represent the best hope of restoring a measure of legitimacy to the system. Gorbachev is faced with unpalatable choices. If he uses force to restore the stability he says is necessary for reform to occur, it will strengthen the position of those most likely to block reform. If he tries to press ahead with reform, he may lose control of the situation, witness breakaway movements in various constituent republics, and precipitate an anti-reform move against him.

Elements of the Craft (2)

The cable implicitly, if not explicitly, brings to bear a number of the analytical tools addressed in chapters 5 and 6. It points to the breakdown of the ideology that had sustained the USSR's ruling class and the effort to create a new one based on reform. It alludes to the violence and intensity of the class conflict then taking place in Soviet society as it discusses the struggle between reformists and conservatives over the future direction of that society. It refers to the country's political culture and the crisis it is undergoing as it discusses the difference between the "situation in which the possession of authority conveyed with it an almost automatic presumption of legitimacy" and "the situation today in which the ability to make authoritative decisions is challenged at every level." It discusses the appeal of specific personalities and both the reasons for and the fragility of that appeal.

Each of these cables provided analysis of a country facing a systemic crisis, but neither was drafted during a specific moment of crisis. Either could have been delayed by days or weeks for further work or deliberation before being submitted without damage to their message or value. That is not the case for the embassy reports covered in the following chapter.

CHAPTER NINE

CASE STUDY II: THE COLLAPSE OF THE SOVIET UNION:
Coup against Gorbachev

In the early hours of August 19, 1991, while Soviet leader Mikhail Gorbachev was vacationing in the Crimea, a self-appointed State Emergency Committee announced that he had taken ill and that the committee had assumed authority. Both the circumstances—remarkably similar to those associated with the coup that had overthrown Nikita Khrushchev in 1964—and the makeup of the committee indicated clearly to those of us at the embassy that Gorbachev was not ill. He had been removed from office, and the committee intended to put an end to the reforms that he had begun. My three-year assignment as head of the political section was almost at an end. I was due to leave Moscow in about two weeks. The ambassador had already departed; our deputy chief of mission had become chargé d'affaires and was heading the embassy pending arrival of the new ambassador, Robert Strauss. There had been a large turnover in the political section that summer, including most of those responsible for analysis of domestic developments. Many of the replacements had been in Moscow for only a few days. All of the embassy staff, including the newest ones, performed with admirable skill and dedication during the ensuing three days.

Embassy reporting during a crisis, particularly a crisis involving a country as important as the Soviet Union, differs in important ways from reporting in more normal times, as one might expect. First, your audience is guaranteed. A round-the-clock task force will be set up in Washington. You will never have more high-level eyes on your work than during a period like this. Second, your competition is fierce. CNN is broadcasting a live feed of what is happening in the streets of Moscow, as are all the other networks that can put together a camera crew. Journalists in Moscow whose work normally appears only in print are now doing double duty as television and radio commentators. The same people impatiently awaiting embassy cables are watching and listening to this live reporting.

If you have developed good skills during your earlier work as a diplomatic political analyst, this is not the time to forget them. Everything will move very quickly. You will be inundated with information and requests for information. A lot of the information available to you will be unsubstantiated, will simply be rumors, or will be total nonsense. The audience at home in your capital will be receiving the same information, rumors, and nonsense. If you are not able to make sense of it in a timely and convincing fashion, you may lose the best opportunity you will ever have to affect your country's foreign policy decisions on something important. Your reporting will be a combination of situation reports (known as "sitreps"), describing what is happening, and analytical efforts, putting what is happening into the relevant context. Style definitely takes a back seat to timeliness in a situation like this. Hopefully, you have honed a sufficiently clear writing style that speed does not translate into unintelligibility. Not that the ambassador and his deputy are going to allow something unintelligible to be transmitted. But they will not appreciate having to act as copy editors, or the delays in reporting that will occur while they copyedit.

The embassy had a remarkable vantage point from which to observe the development of resistance to the coup. One corner of the embassy compound was across the street from a corner of the Russian Parliament building, known locally as the "White House," which became, under Russian President Boris Yeltsin, the center of resistance. Within hours of the coup announcement, people began spontaneously to show up and to construct barricades at the entrances to the White House. As the crowds and the barricades grew, it became clear that the coup leadership faced a level of popular resistance not seen in Moscow since the early days of Communist Party rule.

The American president's initial reaction to this coup was equivocal, perhaps reflecting the fact that it occurred while he, like Gorbachev, was on vacation and had not yet fully consulted with his advisers. His remarks could have been interpreted by the coup leaders as accepting that the coup's success was inevitable and signaling that the United States would work with whoever headed the Soviet Union. Embassy Moscow's initial report on the coup took a different approach. It indicated that the coup could fail under certain conditions, chiefly mass resistance and doubt among the State of Emergency Committee's members that the military would carry out its orders to crush that resistance. This reiterated the dangers of using force against reform that the embassy had pointed out in its December 1990 "Power, Authority and Legitimacy" cable (text in previous chapter):

> The groundswell of public revulsion against the old political structure has made any move that could be interpreted as attempting to preserve or reinstate its power and privileges dangerous for those ordering it. The dangers arise first, from the possibility of mass resistance, à la Romania; and second, from refusal by junior officers and enlisted personnel to carry out orders.

The cable further recommended a policy of no U.S. government contact with the committee and its supporters. The president's statements and the policy the United States subsequently followed strongly opposed the coup and included a freeze in assistance funds, no contact with the putative new government, and conspicuous contact with Yeltsin, who was the most visible symbol of resistance to the coup and the elected leader of the Soviet Union's largest and most important republic.

On the early afternoon of August 21, I was on my way back from Moscow's international airport, where I had put my wife and son on their previously scheduled departure flight, when a traffic tie-up brought my vehicle to a complete stop. Traffic jams of this magnitude were rarer in those days, and the reason for this one soon became clear. From a road to the right, tanks, armored cars, and supporting vehicles of various kinds—a full armored division's worth—emerged and turned, not right into the city, but left out of it. Some of the tanks were buttoned up, but others were open, with crewmen casually sitting atop and waving at the pedestrians on the sidewalk who, understanding instantly what this meant, were cheering, waving, and blowing kisses at them. I recognized, standing with his driver beside his own stopped automobile, Moscow's Mayor Gavril Popov. Walking over, I asked him whether this meant the coup was over. Beaming, he said yes. I then asked him what would happen to the leaders of the coup. "They'll be put on trial," he replied.

I got back to the embassy as quickly as possible and walked into the secure conference room, where newly arrived Ambassador Strauss was getting his first embassy briefing. It was just ending, but the deputy chief of mission asked me whether I wanted to add anything. I said I thought the most useful thing I could say at the moment would be to recount what I had just observed. As soon as I concluded, Strauss stood up and, wily politico that he was, told his deputy to get him connected to Washington on the classified telephone immediately. I left Strauss to do his thing with the highest-ranking official at the White House or the State Department that he could get on the line. I went to do my thing, which was to begin drafting the cable below:

Secret
O 211857Z Aug 91 ZFF4
FM AMEMBASSY MOSCOW
TO SECSTATE WASHDC NIACT IMMEDIATE 2913
WHITEHOUSE WASHDC NIACT IMMEDIATE
SECDEF WASHDC NIACT IMMEDIATE
JCS WASHDC NIACT IMMEDIATE
CIA WASHDC NIACT IMMEDIATE
DIA WASHDC NIACT IMMEDIATE
AMCONSUL LENINGRAD IMMEDIATE
INFO MOSCOW POLITICAL COLLECTIVE IMMEDIATE
USCINCEUR VAIHINGEN GE IMMEDIATE
SECRET MOSCOW 23881
E.O. 12356: DECL:OADR
TAGS: COUP, MOPS, PGOV, PINS, PHUM, CASC, UR
SUBJECT: TFUR01: USSR STATE OF EMERGENCY: ANTI-REFORM COUP COLLAPSES

1. S — Entire Text.
2. BEGIN SUMMARY.
3. The effort to overthrow perestroyka appears to have collapsed in its third day. During these three days the weaknesses of both the junta and its democratic opposition have been apparent. In an event that appears at this point to have been almost unique in Russian history, however, the democratic opposition rallied from a position of complete surprise to offer determined and credible opposition to the weekend coup d'état and apparently to prevail. Whether these forces will be able to remain united once the junta threat is over remains a question mark. END SUMMARY.

THE JUNTA: AN APPEARANCE OF INDECISION AND DIVISION

4. The junta's initial failure to move decisively against Boris Yeltsin proved its most glaring mistake. Either its members were divided among themselves, and therefore indecisive, or they so feared Yeltsin's popularity and so

doubted the loyalty of their forces that they dared not move. Events during the last 24 hours increasingly put the unity of the putschists into question. Yazov reportedly left the committee under unclear circumstances. As of early August 21, Defense Ministry contacts were unable to tell us who either the minister of defense or the chief of staff was. Rumors spread ever more widely that Kryuchkov was also off the committee and that Pavlov was inactive or hospitalized, supposedly because of high blood pressure. Yanayev became an object of derision for the visible shaking of his hands during his public appearances.

5. The loyalty of the military became an ever greater question mark. From the early hours of armor movements into Moscow, Emboffs saw numerous examples of fraternization between military personnel and Muscovites. Elements of at least two armored units went over openly to the RSFSR leadership. Following the bloodshed on the night of August 20/21, the Moscow military commander apologized to the people and said he would remove his troops from the city, according to an unofficial press bulletin.

6. It was generally assumed that the junta had at its disposal loyal, elite forces that could be deployed at a moment's notice to overwhelm the resistance at the RSFSR building. The forces never appeared. Was it lack of will or lack of loyalty that prevented the coup leaders from ordering them into action?

THE RSFSR: SUPPORT PROVED DEEP ENOUGH, EVEN IF NARROW

7. These appearances of junta weakness gave Russian democrats something they had not had at least since Stalin's terror, and perhaps since Lenin's, and something they have rarely had throughout Russian history: the courage to resist and the belief that they could prevail. As we watched the nearest barricades — a mere hundred yards away — home-made and largely hand-made, growing larger by the minute, we could almost see growing with them the determination of these thousands of Russians not to have once more stolen from them the fragile democracy that has been developing here.

8. These people were almost all unarmed and could not, of course, have stood against tanks. But some of them, at least, were ready to fight with whatever they could put their hands on. As people fled the sound of automatic weapon fire last night, running past the embassy compound toward the dubious safety of the crowds at the RSFSR building, they nevertheless

stopped and bodily moved automobiles out into the street to block the armored vehicles they believed were following them.

9.   At the same time, however, even in Moscow, the vast bulk of the population went about its business more or less as usual. Stores were open. Transportation ran more or less normally. The call for a general strike did not produce a dramatic response. The appearance of normalcy remained far greater in most parts of the country than in Moscow or Leningrad, as, so far as we could tell, was the readiness to acquiesce in whatever the power struggle in Moscow yielded. At the same time, the efforts of the coup leaders to use traditional instruments of power — drastically weakened by the Gorbachevian reforms — to mobilize support failed dismally. They were repeatedly either ignored or rebuffed. And the air of normalcy in many areas appears to have been but a surface cover for deep disdain. People who did not openly fight the coup did their best to ignore it, to treat the inhabitants of the Kremlin as irrelevant.

GOING TO GROUND

10. The difference, however, from what would have happened even a few years ago, perhaps even last year, is that there was at least some visible resistance, centered in an individual and an institution invested with the legitimacy of democratic election. The appearance of this resistance, its survival, and the suggestion that the junta was not omnipotent led many who in previous times would automatically have thrown their support to the current residents of the Kremlin to go to ground. Even the expected CPSU Central Committee plenum to oust Gorbachev neither occurred nor was announced, and in the waning hours of the coup CPSU Deputy Secretary General Ivashko reportedly threw his support, in effect, to Gorbachev.

11. Foreign Minister Bessmertnykh went diplomatically ill throughout the three days, surfacing for a press conference immediately after the coup collapsed. His conspicuous absence signaled as clearly as he apparently felt that he dared his attitude toward the putschists. We can only assume that this pattern was ubiquitous throughout the government, as formerly subservient bureaucrats simply failed to carry out the orders they were given. The coup leaders appear to have been generals without troops, both literally and figuratively.

THE FUTURE: VICTORY FOR DEMOCRACY — NOT GORBACHEV

12. This fragile flower of democracy was watered with the blood of martyrs on

the night of August 20. Whatever the wisdom of the actions that led to their deaths, even if they undertook the kind of provocative actions that Yeltsin himself urged against, those who died are now heroes and symbols. The old Russian authoritarian traditions still lie deep-rooted in this society, but the events of the past three days have shown that the courage to defend liberty now exists as well. The challenge to the Russians, and to the other nationalities that inhabit this vast piece of land, will, in the aftermath of the euphoria of these events, be to marry that courage to a greater share of social wisdom than either the moderate reformers, the radical reformers, or the die-hard nationalists has as yet evinced.

13. Democrats face a dilemma. In recent times they were not enamored of Gorbachev, and critical of his apparent deference to the right. The coup forced them to rally to his defense — despite themselves. It is noteworthy that when his possible return from Crimean exile was broadcast to the crowds outside the RSFSR, there was no cheering. Yeltsin's popularity and prestige have, in contrast, skyrocketed. Whether this is a formula for composing the differences between the two men remains to be seen. If the coup ultimately proves unsuccessful. It will surely strengthen the forces of reform, but that may not be enough to hold them together once the threat is over.

IT AIN'T OVER TILL IT'S OVER

14. Finally, while events appear to be moving in the right direction, we remain wary of possible rearguard efforts by the conservatives, who may now calculate that they have nothing to lose by unleashing more violence. This possibility was suggested by the British ambassador, and may be a particular danger in the coming hours and days when the Democrats may be lulled into an early — and premature — sense of victory.

COLLINS[1]

Separate, and shorter embassy situation reports were sent out describing the specific events of this day: my observations about the armored division and my conversation with Mayor Popov, Gorbachev's return to Moscow, the evaporation of the junta. This hastily drafted cable, while affirming what Washington was already hearing from the media—that the coup had collapsed—attempted also to provide some initial perspective on the events of these three days. It pointed out the indecisiveness of the coup leaders;

the role played by Yeltsin and the legitimacy attached to him as the democratically elected leader of Russia; the willingness of thousands of ordinary Russians to risk their lives in support of reform; and the fragility of the coalition, forged by the coup, between the more radical reformers led by the Russian president on the one hand, and the Soviet president and his supporters on the other.

ELEMENTS OF THE CRAFT (3)

The usefulness of the cables in the previous chapter did not depend on how quickly they were drafted or transmitted. Delay of a few days to gather additional impressions, seek further input, and refine the style and concepts would not have mattered significantly. In this case, however, timeliness was paramount. Delays even of hours in transmitting the cable would have put it so far behind the curve of events as to render it significantly less relevant. Events over the next several days were to make clear two significant facts about the changed political landscape: Gorbachev's weakness, particularly vis-à-vis Yeltsin, and the Soviet Union's weakness vis-à-vis its constituent republics, which were all but unanimously declaring their independence, although not at that point defining exactly what independence meant. This analysis addressed the first of these two issues. It did not address the second. We were perhaps too Moscow-focused at that moment. In subsequent days, much of the embassy's reporting was addressed to both of these politically crucial matters.

I would have preferred to omit the final paragraph, which was added by someone else as the cable was being circulated rapidly within the embassy for concurrence before being transmitted. Although I did not agree with the addition and said so, I acquiesced in it because I did not consider that it affected the principal points in the cable and because I wanted to avoid any delays in transmission while debating the point. Working in a bureaucracy means that the craftsman constantly has to make decisions about where to compromise in his work and where not to.

YELTSIN'S VICTORY AND GORBACHEV'S PROBLEMS

In retrospect, it is possible that there is nothing Gorbachev could have done following the coup to reassert his authority. It was clear to those of us at the embassy that his best chance for doing so was during the first twenty-four hours after his return to Moscow and that he missed that chance. The cable below, submitted the day following collapse of the coup, gave our assessment of the changed power equation in Soviet society:

CONFIDENTIAL

O 221958Z AUG 91

FM AMEMBASSY MOSCOW

TO SECSTATE WASHDC IMMEDIATE 2978

WHITEHOUSE WASHDC IMMEDIATE

SECDEF WASHDC IMMEDIATE

JCS WASHDC IMMEDIATE

CIA WASHDC IMMEDIATE

DIA WASHDC IMMEDIATE

AMCONSUL LENINGRAD IMMEDIATE

INFO MOSCOW POLITICAL COLLECTIVE IMMEDIATE

USCINCEUR VAIHINGEN GE IMMEDIATE

E.O. 12356: DECL:OADR

TAGS: COUP, MOPS, PGOV, PINS, PHUM, CASC, UR

SUBJECT: TFUROL: YELTSIN'S VICTORY AND GORBACHEV'S
PROBLEMS

1.   CONFIDENTIAL — ENTIRE TEXT

2.   BEGIN SUMMARY. As Muscovites celebrated in the streets, Soviet
      president Gorbachev began to try to put together the pieces of a
      government that democratic reformers saved, but consider discredited.
      Gorbachev needs to move dramatically to bring into the government
      credible reformers like Shevardnadze and Yakovlev. The defeat of the
      putschists has given him a unique opportunity to sweep away the
      conservative apparatus that has hampered and threatened reform. If he
      does not take that opportunity, he will end the hopes that at least some
      reformers still have that he can be part of the solution rather than part of
      the problem. His public statements and his initial governmental
      appointments, however, give no indication that he understands either the
      opportunity before him or the consequences of not taking it. Tomorrow's
      meeting with the nine republic leaders is likely to bring him sharply up
      against the dramatically changed power equation in this country. END
      SUMMARY.

3.   Russian president Boris Yeltsin and the democratic reformers who defeated
      this week's coup spent the day in public celebration, a celebration that

began in jubilation at the RSFSR building and then, as night fell, moved to KGB and Central Committee headquarters and threatened to get out of control. In scenes reminiscent of East Berlin, Prague, Budapest and Bucharest, crowds in front of KGB headquarters were seeking to bring down the statue of Felix Dzerzhinskiy, founder of the KGB.

4. Soviet president Gorbachev spent most of the day closeted with advisers in an effort to put back together what many reformers openly consider a failed regime. Later, as the crowds were threatening to take over KGB and Central Committee headquarters, Gorbachev was broadcasting an address to the Soviet people and then giving a press conference that with its defense of the CPSU and his commitment to socialism, gave rise to doubts about his grasp of the implications of the events of the past three days.

5. Gorbachev, in our view, now has the opportunity to decisively break the conservative forces that have stalled, fought and imperiled the reform process he undertook. This is not only an opportunity, it is practically a political necessity. Only a sweepingly new team, drawn prominently from the ranks of the reformers who saved his regime, can hope to re-establish the credibility of the central government and forge a workable relationship with republic authorities now more than ever in the ascendancy. Gorbachev must come to terms, and quickly, with a Russian government that saved his regime, and the democratic reform process, but in effect did it by massively usurping the powers of the central government. Having done that, many of its members are not interested in handing those powers back over, and will fight handing them back to a government that is not radically reformed.

6. Unfortunately, the first results of Gorbachev's efforts and his performance before the press do not encourage optimism about his intentions. To the key positions of Minister of Defense, Minister of Interior and KGB chief (all in an "acting" capacity), Gorbachev has appointed, respectively, chief of staff Mikhail Moiseyev, deputy minister of the interior Vasiliy Trushin, and Deputy KGB chairman, and chief of its intelligence department, Leonid Shebarshin. Unless Gorbachev announces clearly that these are only interim and caretaker appointments, he is likely to run into a storm of criticism. All of these men will be considered by reformers as part of the same old pro-communist, anti-reform crowd that has thwarted their efforts and that mounted the coup attempt, exactly the type of "heroes", unheard

from during the three days of crisis, that Yakovlev warned in his public speech today would now emerge and seek to capture Gorbachev.

7. Gorbachev's actions and his public statements today have been a far cry from the calls heard today from prominent reformers — Yeltsin, Khasbulatov, Yakovlev, Popov, Shevardnadze — whose public resistance to the coup is on the public record and is known to all. At the RSFSR building today one or another of these men called for the immediate firing of "hundreds" of military and KGB generals, for the removal of Supreme Soviet chairman Luk'yanov and Foreign Minister Bessmertnykh, for Gorbachev's departure from the CPSU. They poured scorn on those such as Deputy Prime Minister Vitaliy Doguzhiyev who suddenly emerged from the shadows to meet Gorbachev's plane on his return. Another Deputy Prime Minister, Vladimir Scherbakov, came under fierce attack at an August 21 evening press conference in which he lamely attempted to defend the actions of the Council of Ministers during the crisis, and even tried to explain away Prime Minister Pavlov's role in the coup.

8. The mood today among Russian parliamentarians and Muscovites in the street is at once jubilant, proud, angry and vindictive. Gorbachev's credibility among them is already vanishingly small. Unless he puts that jubilation and pride to the service of forming a government of unquestioned reformers, he will quickly find himself the target of the anger and vindictiveness. There are reports in the halls of Moscow radio and television that Gorbachev has told state radio and TV boss Kravchenko to remain at his post. This would put him into direct conflict, a conflict he cannot win, with Yeltsin, who told a wildly cheering crowd of 100,000 today that he had fired Kravchenko.

9. Gorbachev is due to meet at 10 AM tomorrow with the nine republic leaders to discuss what must be done next. Members of Yeltsin's staff have told us that they expect the session to go all day. It is likely to be a difficult one. The putschists acted to prevent signature of the union treaty. Their failure is likely to prevent signature of it as it had been agreed. The republics will now want more power, more control over finances and resources. The weak hand that Gorbachev has to play tomorrow will not have been strengthened by today's developments.

COLLINS[2]

In subsequent days, Gorbachev was to run hard to try to catch up to the changing dynamics of Soviet society. He never succeeded. With his early reform policies, glasnost and perestroika, Gorbachev initiated a conflict of enormous intensity about the nature of Soviet society and the Soviet state. That conflict eventuated in the collapse, not merely of an empire and a country, but of the entire value structure, both professed and actual, on which they were based. The struggle to articulate a new common set of values, a new ideological basis for the Russia of the twenty-first century, continues.

CHAPTER TEN

THE COMPASS AND THE WEATHER VANE

While deputy director of Southern African Affairs, I attended a meeting in Secretary of State George Shultz's office between him and Angolan rebel leader Jonas Savimbi. Savimbi presented the secretary with a carved African walking stick, remarking that in Africa leaders used such sticks to point the way for their people. Smiling, Shultz took the stick, lifted it outward in his right hand and said: "To the right."

A couple of years earlier, while a deputy director for Soviet affairs, I had attended a farewell party at the director's home for our deputy assistant secretary, who was moving on to his next (upward) assignment. The two were friends, and both were relatively young, talented, well liked, and recognized as rising stars in our profession. The deputy received a number of humorous, inexpensive gifts during the party, including a compass from the director. In presenting it, the director told his friend he could use it to point the way and chaffed him about whether his career was more like a compass or weather vane. We all laughed but a little hollowly, since there was perhaps more truth in that chaffing than the director had intended—not just for the deputy, but for all of us.

THE JOB, THE CAREER, AND THE VOCATION

The issues implicit in those remarks are whether and how a diplomat can have an impact on his country's policies and what a diplomat should do when his personal views differ from the policies of the government in power. What you do at those times depends in part on how you view your career. If diplomatic political analysis is a craft, it is a craft that is practiced within the broader context of diplomacy as a profession, just as medicine and the law are professions. Professionals can approach their work in a number of different ways, each of which may be compatible with performing it competently.

Acknowledging that this risks oversimplification, let us consider a profession as a job, as a career, and as a vocation. The professional doing a job puts in as many hours as are required, performs the required duties, regards the work as a way to make a living, and lives for when he is not working. The professional approaching his work as a career puts in as many hours as necessary to get ahead, does what is necessary in order to get noticed, has no policy views of his own, develops skills that enable him to provide superior tactical support for policies others make, and seeks jobs that give him visibility to those who control career advancement. The professional who approaches his work as a vocation puts in as many hours as necessary to do the job the way he thinks it should be done, lets his policy views be known even when they differ from the accepted view, and seeks jobs that he finds personally interesting.

Few enter the diplomatic profession planning to be job holders, but many become just that. A few enter with the mindset of the careerist, planning a rise to the top of the profession without particular concern for policy issues. Those are, however, probably a distinct minority. Most, I suspect, look upon it in their early years primarily as a vocation. As they learn the rules of the game, some of those who have had early success will become careerists; some of those who have not will become job holders.

The careerist becomes very good at providing intellectual content for the policies of those in power and adept at developing tactical steps to carry out those policies. He is a well-oiled and precise weather vane. If he has an internal compass, he keeps it tamped down, perhaps believing that he will be able to employ it effectively once he has reached a sufficiently high level in his profession. And, if he works in a sufficiently obscure functional or geographic area of diplomacy, that may in fact become the case. More likely, however, he will find that he never has the opportunity to put that compass to work or that it has ceased to function, and that he has become the instrument that he has acted as throughout his career—the ultimate weather vane.

While this may seem an indictment of the careerist, it is hardly that simple. The overall political system provides the context within which the diplomat carries out his profession. In authoritarian systems, vocation is not among the choices available to the diplomat. In the former Soviet Union, perhaps some scientists and doctors practiced their professions as vocations but virtually no one else. Some were careerists and members of the Communist Party for the most cynical of reasons. Most simply held jobs and avoided party membership if at all possible. But this did not mean that they were intellectually dead. Many pursued their avocations, their hobbies—music, literature, a craft—with an intensity and degree of knowledge that were remarkable to a Western observer. They created rich intellectual and interpersonal lives for themselves within the space that was of no interest to their rulers. They distinguished clearly between their social/professional and personal personae and experienced no dissonance in espousing one set of social/professional views and entirely different personal views.

Soviet diplomats were the ultimate careerists, espousing the party line with fervor and conviction, and espousing the new party line with equal fervor and conviction as soon as it changed. They did not consider that this reflected negatively upon themselves as human beings. This was their job; they were doing it professionally. In public life, one was expected to be a weather vane; in private life, to have a compass. There was no scorn for behaving as a weather vane publicly; there was for appearing to have no internal compass. As one woman said dismissively of an acquaintance: "He has no opinions of his own. . . . He is like a sausage: what you stuff him with—this he carries around."[1]

Democratic societies differ substantially in how they treat the profession of diplomacy. Public service is generally regarded as a higher status profession in Western Europe than in the United States. Some of the most prestigious institutes and universities in Britain, France, and Germany—the École Nationale d'Administration in France, for example—prepare their students for professional careers that are expected, for the best of them, to culminate in cabinet-level positions. The United States has a far more numerical standard for according prestige: money in business and votes in politics. Business, politics, and money are far more intertwined in the American system than in most democracies. This nexus affects the diplomatic profession significantly.

When I was deputy director for Southern African affairs, the region we covered included ten countries. The United States did not have diplomatic relations with two of them. In six of the remaining eight countries, the ambassador was a political appointee. I remember asking myself at the time what ambassadorships a Foreign Service officer might aspire to if political appointees represented the United States in Lesotho and Swaziland. Worldwide, the distribution of political appointees to career professionals as ambassadors usually runs about 30-70, no matter which political party is in power. Owning a successful used car business in small-town America and giving a noticeable contribution to the president's political campaign are sufficient qualifications for representing the United States as ambassador to a foreign country. In Washington, thirty-something political appointees in their first government jobs are named deputy assistant secretaries, displacing career Foreign Service officers who reached those positions by demonstrating superior ability over more than twenty years of service. It has become standard practice to reserve at least one of the two-to-four deputy assistant secretary positions in each bureau in the State Department for a political appointee.

In democratic societies, a legitimate distinction is generally made between elected officials, who make policy, and public servants, who carry it out. The fact that the use of political appointees to augment public servants, particularly in foreign affairs, is far more widespread in the United States than in most other democracies means that professionals manage foreign affairs within a much more circumscribed framework than in most other democracies. This is a description; whether or not it is also a criticism depends on one's view of what distribution of authority between political leaders and functionaries is "best." This distribution of authority provides the context within which American diplomats pursue their profession. It also affects their choice of pursuing it as a job, a vocation, or a career.

TACTICS, ANOMALIES, AND PARADIGMS

What is the professional diplomat to do when he thinks his government's policies are wrong or counterproductive? A coarse, presumptive answer to that question might depend upon whether he approaches his work as a job, a career, or a vocation. The job holder couldn't care less. The careerist will figure out how to carry out that policy as effectively as possible—and to be seen as doing so. The diplomat practicing a vocation will try to change the policy.

But these distinctions are really too simple. Every professional, in every profession, has to decide which battles to fight. Some State Department officials have made an art form of preemptive capitulation. They never fight, so they never lose. Others fight only when they are certain of victory.[2] A few tilt at every available windmill and gallop off to find new ones if none are in sight.

Those in positions of authority rarely look kindly on analyses that directly challenge their basic outlook. It is normally less career threatening—and, in authoritarian societies, also less personally threatening—to argue about tactics for best meeting the goals of an accepted policy framework than to challenge fundamental tenets of the policy paradigm itself. The successful careerist will become adept at fighting and winning these kinds of tactical battles. It follows, then, that an advisable first step for the diplomatic political analyst who finds himself in disagreement with his government on something is to consider whether the difference is tactical or paradigmatic.

Let us look at chapter 8's case study on the possible collapse of the Soviet Union in this light. The cable made recommendations both on what it called principles and what it called practice (see pp. 85–92). The recommendation on principles did not challenge policies then in effect in large part because there was no overarching policy in effect to challenge. Instead, it recognized that in the fluid situation then existing it could be tempting to pursue short-term advantages at the possible expense of longer-term interests and recommended against that. In the context of the times, that was a general enough—even bland enough—recommendation that almost anyone could agree with it. Its implications following the collapse of the Soviet Union, particularly around the issue of whether to expand NATO eastward, would have been sharper, but by that time a new party held the White House, there was a new staff at Embassy Moscow, and this cable had gone into the archives.

It might seem that the recommendations on practice would, by their nature, involve questions of tactics rather than of paradigm. That is generally correct. The exception in this cable involved the recommendations on arms control negotiations. Those recommendations challenged the paradigm for negotiating arms control agreements, which involved discussions that extended over years, or even decades, between technical and legal specialists so deep in the weeds that they could not recognize a tree, let alone a forest. From our point of view, this paradigm had become an obstacle, and a potentially dangerous one, to achieving the sharp reductions in weapons of mass destruction that the new Soviet leadership appeared ready for. In an effort to ensure a sympathetic audience for our recommendations, rather than an alienated one, we made every effort in the cable to associate the recommendations with existing policies and objectives, even when that involved some stretching of the fabric of reality. The arms control recommendation, because it challenged a paradigm (albeit not one of grand strategy), inevitably required offending the paradigm's supporters, but they were not the audience we sought to convince.

Broadly speaking, there are two ways to challenge an existing policy paradigm: directly, by proposing a new paradigm, and indirectly, by pointing out anomalies in the existing paradigm. (If the reader notices analogies in this discussion to Thomas Kuhn's *The Structure of Scientific Revolutions*, they are not accidental.[3]) Both types of challenge are necessary. An existing paradigm will not change unless there is an alternative available that appears to offer a better way to deal with reality. On the other hand, a new paradigm is not likely to be offered unless a series of credible analyses bring to the surface problems that the old paradigm cannot solve. Just as the scientist carrying out "normal" science uncovers anomalies that may lead to the overthrow of the very scientific paradigm under which he is working, so the diplomatic political analyst may point out problems that implicitly call into question his country's fundamental policies for dealing with a particular country, region, or issue.[4] In pointing out such problems, he may not be (and in fact is probably not) recommending fundamental policy change, but he is contributing to a climate that may become more hospitable to such change. This happens in the foreign policy arena, as in the scientific, because professionals who are respected in their field bring to light anomalies that are recognized as such by the profession as a whole and that stubbornly refuse to fit within the accepted paradigm.[5]

As an example, in 1989 there were still high-level policymakers in Washington who believed that Gorbachev's reforms were aimed essentially at dividing and disarming the West, while creating a more solid domestic base for a renewed Soviet push for world dominance.[6] Embassy Moscow saw things differently and attempted through its political reporting, without challenging this paradigm directly, to demonstrate to Washington that the changes occurring in Soviet society were both real and significant, and could create the conditions for a qualitatively different and improved U.S.-Soviet relationship. We were consciously contributing to the dialogue then going on in Washington about whether the traditional paradigm for understanding the Soviet Union needed to be changed. Ultimately, Gorbachev himself convinced even the most die-hard skeptics by not resisting the breakup of the Warsaw Pact and by accepting decades-old U.S. arms control proposals that encompassed rigorous inspection provisions and required that the Soviet Union cut its forces far more than the United States.[7]

Although as a general rule those in authority are not happy with direct challenges to the existing paradigm, occasionally the climate in the capital may become relatively more hospitable. The most likely time for this is during a change in administration when the new holders of authority are looking for ideas that will distinguish them from their predecessors. This is hardly a no-holds-barred period, however, since the new administration will have taken office on the basis of policy ideas it has already presented to the public. It will bring into positions of authority in the diplomatic establishment many of your intellectual competitors from academia, think tanks, and the legislative branch, and, especially at first, it will regard you with some suspicion since, civil servant or not, you have been working for the previous administration.

It is always essential to understand the paradigms under which you are working. There are at least three. One is the paradigm of the local society that you are attempting to understand. Another is your capital's paradigm for understanding that same society. The third is your personal paradigm for understanding the issues on which you work. During the 1980s, the Western paradigm for interpreting Soviet society included the following all but unchallenged assumptions:

- The Communist Party was in total political control.
- The Soviet Union was an expansionist state with global ambitions and a zero-sum worldview that had to be contained by Western counterpressure.
- The Soviet population was politically indifferent and submissive.
- The military and security apparatus, because of its historical traditions and degree of Communist Party infiltration, would not challenge party control.
- The economy was inefficient but would perform well enough to prevent revolt.
- No dissent existed that was capable of challenging the authority structure.
- Education and economic and technological change might produce pressures for political change but in a time frame measured in decades, if not generations.

This paradigm had proven adequate for understanding Soviet society since at least the early 1950s. Events were shortly to demonstrate that it was no longer adequate. Anomalies existed but were insufficiently understood or were underestimated:

- The upcoming party leadership generation no longer believed in its right to rule.
- Underground culture, for example *samizdat* and political jokes, reflected a popular outlook that was aware, disillusioned, and cynical about those in power.
- The economic infrastructure, starved for decades by demands for military production, was breaking down.
- Efforts to control information flow were stifling scientific and technological progress.
- Nationalism, despite severe repression, still existed in the Soviet republics.

The diplomatic political analyst who explored these or other anomalies would have an interested audience, acceptance as a serious professional, and, more than likely, would be rewarded for his work—and deservedly so, since the identification and analysis of such anomalies would be evidence of high craftsmanship. However, the analyst who took the next step and challenged tenets of the basic paradigm because of these anomalies would likely fare considerably less well. To recognize and report on these anomalies would be one thing; to suggest that any or all of them were sufficiently important to call into question the paradigm would be altogether another.

A higher standard is required of information or interpretations that challenge the accepted paradigm than of those that support it, a standard all but impossible to meet with the information then available. The few nondiplomatic Soviet watchers who did so—we have previously noted the work of Andrei Amalrik and Bernard Levin—were themselves considered anomalies within the profession, more readily seen as examples of the wish becoming the theory than as paradigm breakers. As a diplomatic political analyst, you want your work to be appreciated; you want to be regarded as a skilled craftsman. The danger you face if you move from exploring anomalies to challenging paradigms is that the issue may become not *what* you are saying, but *who* is saying it. You risk being patronized as riding a hobbyhorse of your own choosing or dismissed as a malcontent driven more by personality issues than by substantive ones. You can never win an ad hominem argument and must always try to keep the discussion focused on substance.

QUESTIONS NOT ASKED, ANSWERS NOT WANTED

In *Thinking in Time*, Richard Neustadt and Ernest May look at numerous instances in which American decision makers failed to ask the right questions and a few in which they did. They point out that "illuminating questions are what analysts need most. Decision-makers also need them."[8] I prefer not to ask a question unless I am certain that I want to hear the answer, whatever it may be. Analysts may want to put on the table questions that the political leadership would prefer not be asked. The leadership may be quite content with no answer rather than the risk of an answer it does not like. Or it may consider certain topics simply too politically sensitive for analysis. There exists a certain real, albeit arguably irrational tendency in political capitals to look upon analyses as self-fulfilling prophecies or as wish fulfillment. Asking the question is treated as though you are producing the outcome or desiring the outcome. But political leaders do not always follow this dictum. Most likely because they believe they know the answer and want an "objective" analysis to bear it out, they may ask questions that put both themselves and the analysts in awkward situations. The leaders cannot admit that they want anything other than an objective analysis; the analysts know the answer the leaders want. The question may be withdrawn if the subject is sufficiently sensitive and it becomes known that the analysis is headed in the wrong direction (or the analysis will never be completed), with the tacit agreement of all concerned.

DEEP THROAT OR THE ETHICS OF DISCRETION

Are there ever circumstances that would justify going public with a disagreement over policy matters? Or, to put the question in even more stark terms, are there ever circumstances that would justify leaking classified information because of one's opposition to government policies? The standard answer to the professional diplomat, and from almost all professional diplomats, would most assuredly be no. It is an answer that has weighty arguments behind it. In the United States, Foreign Service officers are appointed by the president to carry out his administration's policies. They are given security clearances and granted access to sensitive information that could have a negative impact on the country's security if released. They have the opportunity to participate in policy formulation from within (although it must be recognized, as previously mentioned, that this opportunity is generally rather limited). In return for accepting these privileges and opportunities, they have taken on an obligation that is both explicit and implicit to carry out their country's policies and not to undermine them either from within or from without. And, of course, they can face both civil and criminal penalties for releasing classified information without authorization.

During a Foreign Service career that spanned over two decades, I knew from press reports and watercooler gossip of a number of leaks of classified information that caused unhappiness on high and led to investigations to try to identify the culprit(s). I can recall only one occasion when I was actually involved in such an investigation. While deputy director for Soviet affairs, I got a phone call from the diplomatic security office requesting an appointment. I assumed it was for a routine security background check on one of my colleagues and readily set up a time. The security official arrived, closed the door to my office, and began asking me about my contacts with a particular diplomat from a Western European country: whether I ever met with him, when, where, etc. In fact, the diplomat in question had come to see me fairly recently. My desk calendar had the date and time of the meeting, and I provided that. As soon as I did so, I realized that the security investigator already had that information and was using it to check my truthfulness.

The questioner remained friendly, but the questions then became more pointed. "Was this diplomat cleared to receive classified information?"

Answer: "I don't know, but I do know that he wasn't cleared to receive classified information from me."

"Are you familiar with [a particular document]?"

"Yes, I cleared it." (The investigator already knew this, since my name was on the document as having cleared it.)

"Did you get a copy of it?"

"I don't remember. I usually get copies of documents I clear, but this is not one I would have kept."

It turned out that this document, which contained sensitive material for the president's meeting with his Western European counterpart, had apparently been handed over to that country without authorization. I do not know whether the offender was ever identified. I heard nothing more about the matter. This leak was to a NATO ally, not to an unfriendly country, but it was still unacceptable.

Leaks occasionally occur because people in the government disagree with the policies being followed or because they believe that the information the public is receiving is misleading or inaccurate. Most diplomatic professionals consider those reasons not good enough and such behavior a lapse in professional ethics. The usual alternatives offered to the diplomat are to express his views within the system or to resign and exercise his rights as a citizen from without. Some years ago, when I was a much younger diplomat, a director general of the Foreign Service laid out these views in an article he titled "The Ethics of Discretion." In an article in response, "Deep Throat or the Ethics of Discretion," I tried to imagine circumstances and rules of behavior that would not merely justify leaking classified or otherwise protected information, but make it the professionally responsible and morally correct thing to do. The Deep Throat reference had to do, of course, with the Watergate scandal during the Nixon presidency. Was Deep Throat justified in his leaks to Bob Woodward and Carl Bernstein? I thought so. An administration that uses illegal means to help ensure its reelection attacks a fundamental principle of the democratic process. I doubt that many people believe that a German diplomat or military officer in World War II who knew about his country's concentration camps and leaked information to the other side would have been acting improperly. But that diplomat or officer would also have validated his decision by putting his life at risk.

There are, then, situations in which leaks are justified, but the examples just given are extreme. What circumstances short of such extremes would be sufficient? In a democratic society, probably few; in an authoritarian society, probably more. If you respect the process, you have to be willing to accept the outcome. One does not have to like the policies of a particular administration, but respect for the process that put it into office implies not using one's privileged position to undermine its ability to govern. In most circumstances, resignation may really be the only ethical alternative.

The most massive leak of classified information that I know of occurred in 2010 when a young U.S. Army enlisted man allegedly provided the text of more than 250,000

State Department cables to WikiLeaks, a nonprofit media organization whose mission is to publish such otherwise unavailable documents. When WikiLeaks made them available on its website, the mainstream media, including the *New York Times* and the *Washington Post*, ran an extensive series of articles drawing from the most dramatic, politically sensitive, and scandalous of the reports. The next chapter includes a discussion of the possible effects of this unprecedented release of embassy reporting on the future of diplomatic political analysis. Setting aside whether the press should publish such leaked materials, which involves issues of press freedom and responsibility that are not the subject of this book, are there other issues involved in this leak that are relevant to the discussion above? Obviously, this was a massive data dump, not a targeted leak intended to express disagreement with a specific policy. It would appear difficult to build an ethically defensible position for such an action unless one begins with the premise either that the United States is the moral equivalent of Nazi Germany and should therefore be opposed by any and all means at the individual's disposal, or that the public has an absolute right to any and all information that its government possesses. I am not unaware of the fact that the United States is capable of serious mistakes of both policy and practice, but nevertheless anyone who argues the first premise lives in a different reality from me. The second premise would allow a more respectable theoretical argument to be built, but its practical effects would be profoundly pernicious. If governments are not able to speak to one another in confidence, then they will speak entirely for public consumption, a sure method of producing in short order a dialogue of the deaf.

There are often ways short of resignation that a diplomat can use to express a principled position on a policy, usually without trashing his career. The clearance process provides one of them. Clearance involves getting a signature of acquiescence on an analytical report or policy recommendation from someone with a bureaucratic stake in the issue at hand. In return for your clearance, you can often negotiate changes in the document to make it reflect your views better. Providing your clearance does not mean that you agree fully with everything in the document, but it does indicate that you do not disagree strongly enough with anything in it to withhold your clearance. Withholding clearance does not necessarily mean that the document will not move forward or that the policy will not come into effect, but it does allow you to dissociate yourself personally from the position or policy. It is best used judiciously, since you run the risk of becoming irrelevant on the issue or of facing retaliation in kind.

During the Vietnam War, the Department of State created a "Dissent Channel" to allow its personnel a means of expressing strongly held views on major policy issues and to ensure that such views were not stifled at the source by the simple means of refusing access to communication channels for them. Regulations require the transmission of Dissent Channel messages and protect their authors from obvious forms of retaliation (e.g., negative performance appraisals), although it can be difficult to guarantee that there will be no negative impacts from more subtle retaliation. Usage of the Dissent Channel has varied substantially over the years. Paradoxically, the more tolerant an administration is of dissent, the less need there is for the Dissent Channel, and the more intolerant it is, the greater may be the reluctance to use it. At a minimum, however, it can help prevent alternate views from being quashed, particularly at embassies abroad. Many chiefs of mission are not reluctant to allow alternative views expressed in reporting from their posts. Even those who are reluctant may prefer to incorporate them into post reporting than have them expressed separately in a Dissent Channel message. This can create negotiating leverage for the analyst who considers his views underrepresented in post reporting.

The best diplomatic professionals, like good sailors, know they need both the weather vane and the compass. The weather vane tells you the course that you can steer. You cannot sail directly into the wind. You must choose a course that allows you to keep your boat under control while heading as closely as possible toward your destination. The compass tells you how far off course the wind is blowing you. It can let you know when you are no longer heading to your destination at all. Keeping that internal compass working while the wind is not under your control and shifting erratically around you is one of a conscientious diplomat's fundamental personal challenges.

CHAPTER ELEVEN

TECHNOLOGICAL CHANGE, THE RISK OF IRRELEVANCE, AND THE CONTINUING NEED

I t is possible that the craft of diplomatic political analysis is dying, although it would be unfortunate if this were so. A variety of developments during the modern diplomatic period, which I would define as the period from the end of World War II to the present, have combined to challenge both the relevance and efficacy of this form of political analysis. These developments span the political, structural, and technological realms. In order to illustrate these changes, we are going to turn our discussion again to imagining the fate of George Kennan's historic Long Telegram sent from Embassy Moscow in 1946 if that same document had been sent in 1990, at the time of Embassy Moscow's "abyss cable." We will then look at the impact of more recent technological changes and imagine the effects of those that will become part of the diplomatic landscape in the near future. But first let us try to put diplomacy into the broadest possible technological context.

TECHNOLOGY AND DIPLOMACY

In the broadest sense, diplomacy is simply a subset of the process of moving people, ideas, and goods from one location to another. During the course of history, technology has produced a few qualitative, revolutionary changes in how things are moved, but not many. Some years ago, I sailed for a week in the Caribbean just before departing for an assignment to Moscow. With good wind, I averaged about six miles (or knots, for the nautically inclined) per hour. Looking out over the sand, the palm trees, and the clear warm waters of the Francis Drake Channel at the end of that vacation, I recognized that my sense of time and space had reverted to the one shared by all of our ancestors until less than 200 years ago. It was jarring to come to grips with the fact that within twenty-four hours I would be in Moscow, a world removed in so many ways from that tranquil island setting.

Six miles per hour—that is about the pace at which people, ideas, and goods could move over any substantial distance for most of human history, whether by land or sea, and then only after the domestication of animals to pull or carry. Techniques and technology could improve this speed—perhaps even double it—for especially valuable things. An emperor, or his orders, could be relayed across his domain. Roman roads were an engineering marvel, but a marvel with a purpose: to move armies, goods, orders, and people across a vast empire. Ultimately, they did not suffice, and the empire was divided to make it more governable. Columbus did not move appreciably faster to the New World than Odysseus to Ithaca, albeit with a better sense of direction.

Not until the 1830s, as the construction of railways began, did it become possible to contemplate a tenfold increase in that rate of movement, to sixty miles per hour. Over the next several decades, that promise was achieved, and average people and goods, not just kings and silks, could move across the earth at speeds that a generation or two before would not have been conceivable. Interestingly, despite all of humanity's advances since, that tenfold increase remains close to the best achievable speed for moving goods and people over land. Yes, as in earlier eras, techniques and technology—the bullet train, the autobahn, the BMW—can double that in exceptional instances, but not on average.

At about the same time, discoveries were being made that eventuated in the commercially successful telegraph messaging system. By the 1860s, information could literally move across continents at the speed of light, although relays and the operator limitation of forty to fifty words per minute limited the speed in practice and rendered the technology not especially practical as a means of transmitting complex ideas.

The next tenfold increase in the movement of people and goods became a widespread reality only in the post–World War II era, with the commercialization of jet flight. That 600-mile-per-hour limitation remains generally in effect today, although once again technology and techniques can double that for high-value goods and people, as the Concorde demonstrated. Thus far, only nuclear warheads have been considered sufficiently valuable cargo to be transported at the speed of the next tenfold increase in movement. During this period as well, electronic communications became sufficiently sophisticated to allow the secure transmission of complex ideas and detailed information.

As the limits of time and space have decreased, so too has the diplomat's room to maneuver. Sovereigns have always wanted to ensure that their representatives carry out their wishes. Diplomats act, therefore, on the basis of instructions. Smart diplomats do their best to write their own instructions before departing their capitals.[1] It is not unusual for their negotiations at home over their instructions to be more difficult than their negotiations abroad with their foreign counterparts. But instructions once intended to last through an entire negotiating process can now be revised daily. They have changed from high-level policy guidelines to far more detailed blueprints. In addition, negotiations can be and increasingly often are carried out by representatives visiting from capitals, rather than by ambassadors in the host country. These changes have had significant impact not only on instructions flowing from capital to embassy, but also on information, analysis, and recommendations flowing from embassy to capital.

EMBASSY REPORTING, FROM CONTAINMENT TO COLLAPSE

Kennan's 1946 Long Telegram and the 1990 Embassy Moscow cable that served as a case study in chapter 8 may serve as convenient reference points for a discussion of how and whether embassy reporting can contribute significantly to the formation of wiser and more effective U.S. policies in the foreign arena. Kennan's analysis directed itself to U.S. policy for dealing with the long-term threat posed by a powerful Soviet state ideologically antithetical to the United States. The later Embassy Moscow cable directed itself to post-containment American policies for dealing with the possible end of that Soviet state.

Between 1946 and 1990, technological, bureaucratic, and information developments made it far more difficult for embassy dispatches to have a significant impact on foreign policy formation. Those trends have since continued, even accelerated. Many of the technological developments are obvious, but their impact on embassy reporting warrants some elaboration. We pointed out in chapter 3 that in 1990 Kennan's dispatch would not have been referred to as the "Long Telegram"; it would have been called "Embassy Moscow cable number 23,603." Obviously, the great majority of those 23,000-plus cables concerned routine administrative or consular matters and would have been labeled and distributed accordingly. They would not have been competitors for the audience he sought. Nevertheless, a staggering increase in the volume of substantive analytical dispatches took place over that time period, not only from Moscow, but from a vastly expanded diplomatic establishment around the world.

At the same time, the Washington audience for Embassy Moscow reporting expanded greatly. But here, too, a paradox exists, for that large audience would consist not of passive consumers of his brilliance, but of multitudes of producers of their own analytical efforts. We discussed them in chapters 3 and 4 as the diplomatic political analyst's

audience and competitors. Between 1946 and 1990, the Washington governmental foreign affairs apparatus grew exponentially: CIA, DIA, INR, NSA, NSC—each staffed
with large numbers of energetic governmental officials with a vested interest in getting
their views, not Kennan's, in front of senior policymakers.

In 1946, Kennan was deputy chief of mission in Moscow. His Long Telegram was
a departure-from-post summing-up of his views, addressed as a personal message from
him to the secretary. That would not have happened in 1990 or thereafter. By then,
such departure messages were rare, albeit not unheard of. They were never addressed to
the secretary unless authored by the ambassador. If Kennan had written such a message
in 1990, he would probably have addressed it to the assistant secretary for European
affairs. The assistant secretary, if sufficiently impressed, might have passed it upward or
even mentioned it personally to the secretary at a staff meeting. The chances that the
secretary would have actually read it were vastly smaller in 1990 than in 1946. The embassy's 1990 abyss cable, though authorized and approved by the ambassador, represented the views of the embassy, rather than the personal views of the ambassador.[2] As
such, it had even less chance of reaching the office of the secretary, or the offices of any
of the Seventh Floor principals, and no chance at all unless someone in the department
made an unusual effort to call it to their attention. That said, higher-ranking department
personnel do have staffers specifically tasked to ensure that they see significant reports,
while filtering out those that do not merit their attention. Even in this era of electronic
movement of information, there is a person in the machine at key points.

IMPACT OF THE INFORMATION AGE
Technological developments since 1990 have increased the challenge of maintaining
the relevance and independence of diplomatic political analysis. Even in 1990, major
embassies had classified telephone connections with Washington. Since 1990, classified
e-mail has become an exponentially growing means of communication between the
capital and the field. The positive side of this is that it allows a more personal and informal channel of communication, which can be particularly desirable between an embassy and its geographic desk. It allows either side to alert the other of issues or problems
that it may not want to put into a more formal communication. It would, for example,
be a desirable means for the desk to alert the embassy that the assistant secretary was
personally interested in a particular development in the host country and had asked at
that morning's staff meeting whether there was an embassy report on it. There are any
number of good reasons why an embassy might not have reported on that development,

but any embassy would be grateful to know that someone at the assistant secretary level or higher had expressed an interest in it. An embassy furnished that knowledge that did not make it its business to get in a report on the subject pretty quickly would be profoundly asleep at the switch.

The example above pretty clearly demonstrates that these technological developments afford opportunities to keep embassy reporting *more* relevant to concerns in the capital. But this is a two-edged sword. It increases the pressure on embassy reporting to adopt the capital's paradigm for understanding what is happening locally. This vitiates what ought to be one of the key values of embassy reporting—having capable people on the ground who can independently assess local developments. Efforts to influence the tone and content of embassy reporting can occur for a variety of reasons, including, as we have noted above, some good ones. One less desirable manifestation is the attempt to enlist embassy analyses on one or the other side in a policy dispute within the capital. Secure telephonic or e-mail communications provide a relatively discreet medium for doing this. There will be times when an embassy will be only too ready to lend its weight to one or the other side in such a policy dispute. There will be other times when it would prefer to stay out of the fray or finds itself favoring a view other than that held by those seeking its help. It is immeasurably more difficult to do that now, after an informal, personal request from someone important to the embassy in the capital, than it was prior to the advent of these modes of communication.

Perhaps the most pernicious effect of these technological developments is a tendency to send drafts of embassy dispatches that might prove controversial to the capital by classified e-mail for a sort of pre-clearance by interested offices. The basic question being asked is a prototypical careerist question: will this ruffle any feathers? If the response is yes, the dispatch may never be sent, or its feather-ruffling edges smoothed off before formal transmission. This would not have been an issue prior to the advent of these technological developments. An embassy might well have engaged in some self-censorship, but it would not have had the means to submit its ideas for prior censorship by persons in the capital. What would have happened, for example, to Jack Matlock's cable suggesting that Leonid Brezhnev might be preparing a move against Soviet Communist Party general secretary Khrushchev in the era of classified e-mail? I am not suggesting that either the political counselor to whom he reported or the ambassador would have sent the cable in as a classified e-mail before submitting it, but some political counselors and some ambassadors would. If they had, the geographic desk would have told the embassy that Ambassador Thompson wanted it to cease engaging in "silly Kremlinology." It is one thing to hear afterward that a particular highly placed and influential individual did not like an embassy analysis; it is an altogether different thing to hear that prior to submitting the analysis through normal channels. A lot of political counselors and a lot of ambassadors would hesitate under those circumstances.

The State Department tends to lag behind other elements of the foreign affairs and intelligence bureaucracy in adopting new technology. In large part, this is simply because it lacks the resources to move more quickly. Nevertheless, the political analyst today operates in a rapidly changing technological environment. The department participates in a classified Internet system called "SIPRnet" ("Secure Internet Protocol network"). Messages designated "SIPDIS" ("Secure Internet Protocol Distribution") become accessible to all who have access to this classified system. Many embassies have set up classified websites, referred to as a "web presence" on which they can post their reports and analyses for review by anyone who can access the website. The Department's "SMART" ("State Messaging Archival Retrieval Toolset") system puts cables directly into recipients' computer in-boxes (currently based on Outlook). Cables, in fact, are no longer simply cables. They are organizational authority messages (from an entity such as an embassy); "MDA," or "messages directly addressed," which are automatically put into the computer in-box of a specific designee or designees, as well as automatically archived; and "FTR," or "for the record messages," which are submitted directly to the archives and not viewed by an individual unless specifically researched. Communication technology makes these changes possible, but political factors made them essential. Criticisms of the intelligence community's failure to share information in the period up to the 9/11 attacks led to a variety of reform proposals. The 9/11 Commission endorsed an earlier recommendation that a "culture of distribution" be created in the intelligence community, with "distributable products . . . created at the outset."[3] Although most of the State Department is not considered part of the intelligence community, it seems likely that those recommendations also informed the department's own communications revamping.

E-mail exchanges, either classified or unclassified, can still be used for informal communication, but any addressee can mark an e-mail message "FTR," which puts it into the archives. Instant messaging has reached the State Department, with a high (or classified) and a low (or unclassified) side. IMs can be converted to e-mail, which can then be archived. Some posts have Blackberry servers, which allow visitors to receive unclassified e-mails and to put search alerts in the SMART system for messages on specific subjects or automatic alerts for high-precedence messages.

Just as the combination of post-9/11 political factors and technological advances changed traditional message formats and distribution methodologies, so in related fashion they have changed one of the most cherished tenets of the traditional security system for handling classified information. For many years, "need to know" governed one's access to such information. The State Department's information systems now emphasize "need to share." In practical terms, this means that any cleared employee or contractor can search the State archives for information on any subject. This accords with what one observer sees as a common theme in recent intelligence reform proposals, a dedication to the free flow of information in a more flexible networked infrastructure.[4] Obviously, this does not mean every message on every subject is available to every employee. Restriction designators can still be used to limit access to the more sensitive communications. One of the still unanswered questions is how the change from need to know to need to share will affect the use of restriction indicators. Will they tend to proliferate so as to limit this open access to the more mundane communications?

The unauthorized WikiLeaks release will have a variety of consequences and may lead to a walking back of some of the "need to share" principles established after 9/11. Clearly, if they allow a young enlisted soldier to access and release that volume of material, most of it classified, something needs to be changed. The usual bureaucratic kneejerk reaction would be to restrict information sharing, but this brings with it the danger of recreating the information stove-piping that contributed to the 9/11 intelligence failure. At a minimum, obviously something needs to be done about separating the ability to access information from the capability of releasing it.

From the embassy reporting standpoint, this event poses still another challenge to the candor that is so essential to good analysis. First, it may make the analyst's sources less likely to be open for fear that their remarks may become public knowledge. We noted in chapter 7 that the State Department considers the persuasiveness and value of embassy analysis to depend in substantial part on the credibility of its sources. If those sources dry up or are not identified in reports, the value of the reports to policymakers will decrease. Second, the release of these cables adds further to the pressures, real or imagined, on embassies to not say anything in their reports that could conceivably offend anyone. Fostering an environment that encourages reporting candor in the face of these technological and political developments will be an ongoing challenge, both at embassies and within the State Department.

Other technological developments conceivably call into question the very need for traditional written analysis. For example, some embassies now have secure video-conferencing capabilities. The department has not yet introduced a secure webcam system, but this will no doubt come with time and money. It will mark a major change in the way political analysis is done from posts abroad, putting a premium on oral briefing skills and perhaps further limiting the impact of traditional written diplomatic political analysis. The fundamental problem with this in the field of political analysis is the same as Lee Iacocca identified in business years ago: "In conversation, you can get away with all kinds of vagueness and nonsense, often without even realizing it. But there's something about putting your thoughts on paper that forces you to get down to specifics. That way, it's harder to deceive yourself—or anybody else."[5]

There is, however, no point in bemoaning these technological changes. In the first place, they have positive aspects as well as negative ones; perhaps more positive than negative. In the second place, they are not going away. If technological changes do increasingly substitute oral briefings for written analysis, the challenge for future craftsmen will be how to retain in their oral briefings as much of the desirable characteristics of embassy political analyses as possible: independence, first-hand information, cultural understanding, and linguistic skill.

BUREAUCRATIC SURVIVAL AND PARADIGM CHANGE

Every diplomatic service is, or is part of, a bureaucracy. The skills needed for survival and success in a bureaucracy tend to be those of a careerist, as we defined them in chapter 10. The Department of State has perhaps been more creative than most bureaucracies in trying through organizational and structural means to accept and encourage differing viewpoints on policy issues. It has established an office, the Open Forum Panel, with the mission of bringing outside views to the attention of department personnel and encouraging and monitoring the submission of dissenting views on policy issues. It has created a Dissent Channel, which, in principle at least, provides a means for personnel to be heard who cannot get their views put forward through normal channels. Despite this, the real world choices for someone who differs from established policy views are difficult. Promotion panels make decisions based on an individual's personnel file, which contains evaluation reports, awards, etc. All of this is on the record and accessible to the individual concerned. Desirable, career-enhancing jobs, on the other hand, depend much more on one's "corridor reputation"—what your peers and superiors say about you in informal conversations. Promotion panels know what the important jobs are. Over time, if you are not getting them, you will be promoted much less quickly than someone who is, even if both sets of personnel files are otherwise indistinguishable.

This is reality. It is part of life in any bureaucracy. Structural fixes can have at best only limited impact on it. The difficult but ultimately more promising avenue is to keep promoting attitudinal changes, which may well be the most important contribution that structural fixes make. Each of us creates his own paradigm for understanding the world around him. In addition, we have collective paradigms, bureaucratic or cultural, from which we draw and to which we contribute. The real issue is not our paradigms, but how we view the anomalies in the paradigms and how we treat those pesky colleagues who uncover and point them out. We need not view them automatically with awe and their discoverers with respect. Many supposed anomalies turn out to be nothing more than mistakes and their discoverers mistaken. It is right to challenge a proclaimed anomaly, to require that it be submitted to appropriate proofs. The emotion behind the challenge should arise, however, not from fear that the paradigm may be under attack, but from excitement that perhaps something new has been discovered.

IN CONCLUSION: CRAFT AND CALLING

Lorenzo Ghiberti spent most of his adult life working on his two sets of doors for the Baptistery of St. John in Florence. Trained originally by his father as a goldsmith, Ghiberti became one of the Renaissance's consummate artists. He was paid well for his work. The first set of doors, which took him two decades to complete, reportedly cost the equivalent of the Florentine defense budget for one year. Little wonder that he was prepared to sign a contract for the second set, an even more magnificent achievement that took three decades and that Michelangelo would coin "the gates of Paradise." The workshop that he established to carry out these projects trained craftsmen who became some of the finest artists of the Renaissance: Donatello and Masolino, among others. We might take a moment to reflect on the many others in that workshop during those fifty years who made those doors possible: craftsmen, doing a job, drawing a salary.

Today's Baptistery door projects are not to be found in the arts, but in the sciences: flights to the Moon or Mars; supercolliders; Hubble telescopes. The craftsmen in these projects often must wait as many years as Ghiberti's to see the fruits of their labor. And most of these craftsmen will be equally unknown to history.

We began this book by defining diplomatic political analysis as a craft, containing some elements of science and, at times, a bit of art. At the end of his work, there will be no Baptistery doors for the practitioner of this craft, no artistic marvel for humankind to admire over the centuries. There will be no Hubble telescope opening new vistas into an awesome universe. It would be difficult to believe that most of Ghiberti's craftsmen and most of the Hubble workers were there just to make a living. Most surely shared a common purpose: to create something of which they might be proud. Can the diplomatic political analyst find something in his craft to provide an emotional equivalent? I think he can.

Artistic marvels and scientific achievements are monuments to what humanity is capable of at its best. But, at the risk of restating a cliché, it remains true that the most difficult and baffling issue man faces is how to understand his fellow man and how to live at peace with him. This has never been as important as in the modern diplomatic era, when we have created more than one technology that could render this species extinct. The diplomatic political analyst is among those at the cutting edge of this issue. He has the opportunity to bring his knowledge and his skill to bear on understanding—and on conveying to others at home who do not share his craft—how people with a different language, history, and culture see the world. He has the opportunity to suggest means for bringing their interests into harmony with those of his own country.

It would be naïve to think that even perfect understanding, perfectly conveyed, would eliminate international conflict. Interests differ and conflict is inevitable, sometimes even desirable. The able practitioner of his craft in Germany in the 1930s should probably have been telling his government that no concession could bring peace, and perhaps he was. More works of art have been melted down for cannonballs in history than swords turned into plowshares. Sound judgment and good advice do not always carry the day in international affairs. The artist has no control over his work once it leaves his hand. The scientist cannot predict what use will be made of his discovery. The pursuit of beauty and the pursuit of understanding must be seen as worthy ends in themselves. In the words of Conrad, "The moral side of an industry . . . is the attainment and preservation of the highest possible skill on the part of the craftsmen. Such skill, the skill of technique, is more than honesty; it is something wider, embracing honesty and skill and rule in an elevated and clear sentiment, not altogether utilitarian, which may be called the honour of labour. It is made up of accumulated tradition, kept alive by individual pride, rendered exact by professional opinion, and, like the higher arts, it is spurred on and sustained by discriminating praise."[6] So, in his own way, the craftsman in our field must pursue his work, understanding that he does not control the outcome, contributing what he can, as best he can, to a worthy endeavor.

Notes

CHAPTER 1. WHAT IS POLITICAL ANALYSIS AND WHY IS IT A CRAFT?

1. *The American Heritage Dictionary of the English Language, Fourth Edition* (Boston: Houghton Mifflin, 2003).

2. There have generally been two criteria for access to specific classified information: having the appropriate security clearance and having a specific reason for needing to know the information in question. While for most "routine" classified material the "need to know" is not a significant bar to access, it becomes a greater issue with regard to more sensitive information. The implications of this will be discussed in more depth later, as will modifications of the "need to know" doctrine that have resulted from a combination of technological developments and the September 11, 2001, attack on the United States.

3. I want to stipulate that in almost every place where I use the term "his," I mean "her or his." I hope the reader will forgive me for choosing stylistic simplicity over gender neutrality.

4. Edward T. Hall, *Beyond Culture* (Garden City, NY: Anchor Press/Doubleday, 1976).

CHAPTER 2. THE OBJECTIVES OF DIPLOMATIC POLITICAL ANALYSIS

1. This is how it is supposed to work. The author recognizes that in the real world these lines may be crossed, either accidentally or deliberately.

2. This is cable-speak for embassy officer. It is generally considered bad form to identify oneself by name in embassy cables, although titles may be used for more senior embassy officers (e.g., political counselor).

3. Steve Kashkett, recipient of the award in 1992, responding in 2008 to the author's questionnaire on diplomatic political analysis (hereafter cited as "author's questionnaire").

CHAPTER 3. THE AUDIENCE

1. And sometimes you are surprised. In my case, the assistant secretary personally complimented me on my analytical efforts, and the embassy nominated me for the department's annual political reporting award, pleasant experiences for an officer on his second political assignment abroad.
2. We will discuss what these terms mean for diplomatic political analysis in a later chapter.
3. Stan A. Taylor and David Goldman, "Intelligence Reform: Will More Agencies, Money, and Personnel Help?," *Intelligence and National Security* 19, no.3 (Autumn 2004): 416–435, 420.
4. I have been told by someone then involved in these matters at the State Department that the intelligence community was unanimous in its judgment on the likelihood that Iraq had a chemical or biological weapons program. Two analysts in the INR Bureau disagreed with the assessment that Iraq had an active nuclear weapons program.
5. X (Kennan, George F.), "The Sources of Soviet Conduct," *Foreign Affairs* 25 (July 1947): 566–582.

CHAPTER 4. THE COMPETITION

1. Strobe Talbott, "Globalization and Diplomacy: A Practitioner's Perspective," *Foreign Policy* 108 (Fall 1997): 69. Since Talbott was speaking on an open telephone line, he had to depict the conversation as unclassified, no matter what he was discussing.
2. Amb. Daniel C. Kurtzer, S. Daniel Abraham Visiting Professor of Middle East Policy Studies, Woodrow Wilson School of Public and International Affairs, Princeton University. Ambassador Kurtzer is a former career Foreign Service officer and received the Director General's Award for Reporting in 1985. The text quoted is from his response to author's questionnaire.
3. "Food No Longer Reaches City," *Washington Post,* December 23, 1990; "Soviet Neighbors Brace for Refugees," *Washington Post,* December 23, 1990; "Poland, Others Forecast Flood of Soviet Refugees," *Washington Post*, November 15, 1990; "Western

Europe Braces for Migrant Wave," *New York Times*, December 14, 1990; "Food Shortages Cause Desperation in Moscow," *New York Times,* November 27, 1990.

4. Bill Keller in the *New York Times* and David Remnick in the *Washington Post* were two of the journalists who got this story right. They reported on the record harvest, pointed out the rampant waste that was endemic to the Soviet agricultural system, and cited distribution breakdowns that could produce local shortages.

5. Jack Matlock, *Autopsy on an Empire* (New York: Random House, 1995), 437.

6. Mark Foulon, former deputy under secretary of commerce, former career Foreign Service officer and recipient of the Director General's Award for Reporting in 1990. Response to author's questionnaire.

CHAPTER 5. THE ANALYST'S PERSONAL TOOLKIT

1. This is not false modesty. I am not gifted at foreign languages. With difficulty, I became somewhat adequate in Russian and a bit better than adequate in French. I regarded my colleagues more gifted in this area with admiration and a bit of envy.

2. Amb. Jack Matlock, personal communication, November 30, 2007.

3. For more on how cultural differences affect Russian negotiating style, see my book, *Negotiating with the Soviets* (Bloomington, IN: Indiana University Press, 1989).

4. Based on *Caesar's Commentaries on the Gallic War,* literally translated with explanatory notes by Edward Brooks Jr. (New York: David McKay, 1895), 1. On page ix of his introduction, Brooks indicates that "the purpose of this translation is to afford those who are unable to read 'The Commentaries' in the original Latin an opportunity of making themselves familiar with Caesar's matchless style." A literal translation does not always do justice to that style. In the passage quoted, I have put Brooks's translation into more contemporary English by eliminating a few words that we would consider extraneous and by making a few changes in word order and syntax. I believe these changes give the modern reader a better sense of the "force and clearness of expression" that Brooks admires and that Caesar's contemporaries appear to have appreciated.

5. Edward Gibbon, *The History of the Decline and Fall of the Roman Empire* (London: Folio Press, 1983), 31.

6. Betty Radice, introduction to ibid., 15.

CHAPTER 6. THE ANALYTICAL TOOLS

1. *American Heritage Dictionary.*

2. See Dick Combs, *Inside the Soviet Alternate Universe* (University Park: Pennsylvania State University Press, 2008), especially 173–197, for a well-informed discussion of the changes in the leadership mindset during this period.

3. Thomas Kuhn, *The Structure of Scientific Revolutions* (Chicago: University of Chicago Press, 1962), 64.

4. Ibid., 52.

5. Ibid., 84.

6. Ibid., 91–95.

7. Ralf Dahrendorf, *Class and Class Conflict in Industrial Society* (Stanford, CA: Stanford University Press, 1959), 210–213, 236–240.

8. Ibid, 239.

9. Kuhn, *Structure*, 137. As, Kuhn argues, do scientific textbooks, in which "science . . . comes to seem largely cumulative." On the same page, Kuhn recognizes that scientists are "not, of course, the only group that tends to see its discipline's past developing linearly toward its present vantage."

10. Kuhn, *Structure*, 137–138.

11. Andrei Amalrik, *Will the Soviet Union Survive until 1984?* (New York: Harper & Row, 1970). Bernard Levin's August 1977 article in *The Times* (London) is reprinted in *The National Interest*, no. 31 (spring 1993), 64–65. Amalrik believed that an external event—a war with China—would be the trigger, whereas Levin considered that an internal reform effort would do it.

12. Richard A. Best, Jr., "What the Intelligence Community Got Right about Iraq," *Intelligence and National Security* 23, no.3 (June 2008): 289–302.

13. As happened with the National Intelligence Estimate that concluded Iran had abandoned its nuclear weapons program in 2003 ("Iran Ended Nuclear Arms Bid in 2003, U.S. Intelligence Review Concludes," *Washington Post*, December 4, 2007).

14. Sarah E. Kreps, "Shifting Currents: Changes in National Intelligence Estimates on the Iran Nuclear Threat," *Intelligence and National Security* 23, no.5 (October 2008), 608–628, 612.

15. Archie Brown, ed., *Political Culture and Communist Studies* (New York: M. E. Sharpe, 1985), 156.

16. Smith, *Negotiating*, 5.

17. Interfax, Moscow, January 23, 2009, citing a poll conducted by the Levada Center January 16–19, 2009.

CHAPTER 7. CRITERIA FOR SUPERIOR REPORTING: THE STATE DE-
PARTMENT VIEW

1. This may have been a matter of personalities, rather than of bureaucracies, since in 2010 when I sought information for a possible follow-up to this book, the department was quite helpful in providing the information I requested.

2. The author could not find information on the winners for 1991, 1999, 2003, and 2005. The information that follows is not, therefore, inclusive of the 1984–2007 period but of the twenty awards issued during that period on which information is available in the public sector.

3. *State* magazine, August/September 1987, 15.

4. Foulon, response to author's questionnaire.

5. Kashkett, response to author's questionnaire.

6. Kurtzer, response to author's questionnaire.

7. Foulon, response to author's questionnaire.

8. Released in part B1, 1.4 (D), U.S. Department of State, Review Authority: Sharon E. Ahmad, Date/Case ID: 25 Aug 2008, 200803296.

9. Released in part B1, 1.4 (D), U.S. Department of State, Review Authority: Sharon E. Ahmad, Date/Case ID: 25 Aug 2008, 200803296.

10. *State* magazine, October 1993, 15.

11. Kashkett, response to author's questionnaire.

CHAPTER 8. CASE STUDY I: THE COLLAPSE OF THE SOVIET UNION:
EARLY EMBASSY MOSCOW VIEWS

1. Kurtzer, response to author's questionnaire.

2. Foulon, response to author's questionnaire.

3. Released in full and decaptioned, U.S. Department of State, Review Authority: Theodore Sellin, Date/Case ID: 28 Feb 2007, 200605403.

4. Personal communication from Amb. Jack Matlock to the author, September 30, 2007.

5. The reader should understand that these recommendations did not arise out of thin air. Some of them reiterated key points in the four-point agenda that stemmed back to the Reagan presidency; others had been made previously by the embassy and/or by the ambassador personally. See, for example, Matlock, *Autopsy*, 148–149, 188–189. We considered that emerging conditions gave them a new urgency.

6. Personal communication from Amb. Jack Matlock to the author, November 30, 2007.

7. Released in full and decaptioned, U.S. Department of State, Review Authority: Theodore Sellin, Date/Case ID: 05 FEB 2008, 200702478. The ambassador was not in Moscow when this cable was transmitted. James Collins, the deputy chief of mission, was in charge of the embassy in the ambassador's absence and the cable therefore went out over his name.

CHAPTER 9. CASE STUDY II: THE COLLAPSE OF THE SOVIET UNION: COUP AGAINST GORBACHEV

1. Released in full, U.S. Department of State, Review Authority: Theodore Sellin, Date/Case ID: 05 FEB 2008, 200702478.
2. Released in full, U.S. Department of State, Review Authority: Theodore Sellin, Date/Case ID: 05 FEB 2008, 200702478.

CHAPTER 10. THE COMPASS AND THE WEATHER VANE

1. Margaret Mead and Rhoda Metraux, eds., *The Study of Culture at a Distance* (Chicago: University of Chicago Press, 1953), 213.
2. If bureaucratic battles are viewed as another form of warfare, this is an approach with ancient wisdom to support it. The "victories [of the expert] in battle are un-erring. . . . He acts where victory is certain, and conquers an enemy that has already lost." (Sun-Tzu, *The Art of War* [London: Folio Society, 2007], 90.) Of course, Sun-Tzu's expert creates conditions that make victory certain. He does not wait passively for a battle to come his way that he is certain to win.
3. See chapter 6, pp. 49–50.
4. In this context, the cables by Steven Kashkett presented in chapter 7 clearly illustrated anomalies with potential implications for the U.S. paradigm for thinking of the Middle East peace process.
5. Kuhn, *Structure*, 96.
6. Matlock, *Autopsy*, 183.
7. There were humorous elements in the "I can't believe this is happening" reaction among some longtime U.S. arms control and counterintelligence specialists. They appeared to realize with dismay and for the first time that the obligations in these proposals were indeed, as the proposals stated, reciprocal, and, yes, if we wanted inspectors on Soviet bases, Soviet inspectors would have to be allowed on ours.
8. Richard E. Neustadt and Ernest R. May, *Thinking in Time: The Uses of History for Decision-Makers* (New York: Free Press, 1986), 149.

CHAPTER 11. TECHNOLOGICAL CHANGE, THE RISK OF IRRELEVANCE, AND THE CONTINUING NEED

1. Castlereagh's negotiations with the British cabinet before departing on his post-Napoleonic negotiations on the Continent illustrate this. See Henry Kissinger's *A World Restored: Metternich, Castlereagh and the Problems of Peace, 1812-22* (Boston: Houghton Mifflin, 1957).

2. Matlock, *Autopsy*, 405. When he considered it important to do so, Ambassador Matlock did draft his personal views for Washington attention (see, for example, ibid. 185–189), and he had periodic opportunities to meet with the president and the secretary.

3. Calvert Jones, "Intelligence Reform: The Logic of Information Sharing," *Intelligence and National Security* 22, no. 3 (June 2007): 384–401, 390.

4. Ibid., 388.

5. Lee Iacocca, *Iacocca* (New York: Bantam, 1984), 47.

6. Joseph Conrad, *The Mirror of the Sea* (London: The Folio Society, 2005), 45–46.

Annotated Reading List

In keeping with the orientation of this book, this reading list focuses primarily, although not exclusively, on works by professional diplomats. Many of them are included in the suggested reading list of the Association for Diplomatic Studies and Training.

U.S. DIPLOMATIC HISTORY
General Surveys

Eicher, Peter D. *"Emperor Dead" and Other Historic American Diplomatic Dispatches.* **Washington: Congressional Quarterly Books, 1996.** A fascinating selection of over 260 dispatches from 1776 to the Vietnam War era, most taken directly from originals in the National Archives, many previously unpublished or inaccessible.

Cold War Era

Hart, Parker T. *Two NATO Allies at the Threshold of War—Cyprus: A Firsthand Account of Crisis Management, 1965–1968.* **Durham, NC: Duke University Press, 1990.** An insider's case study of crisis management, skillful diplomacy, and the shuttle diplomacy of Cyrus Vance.

Kirk, Roger, and Mircea Raceanu. *Romania versus the United States: Diplomacy of the Absurd, 1985–1989.* **New York: St. Martin's Press, 1994.** A revealing insiders' account of the deteriorating special relationship between the United States and Romania in the last years of Nicolae Ceauşescu by the two chief diplomatic actors in the drama.

Matlock, Jack. *Autopsy on an Empire.* New York: Random House, 1995. The definitive account of the events leading up to the collapse of the Soviet Union, written by the U.S. ambassador in Moscow from 1987 to 1991.

Miller, Robert H. *Vietnam and Beyond: A Diplomat's Cold War Education.* Lubbock: Texas Tech University Press, 2002. The exceptional "hands-on" knowledge and critical evolution of a career diplomat who worked on America's unsuccessful Vietnam venture and its aftermath for nearly one-third of his Cold War–spanning career.

Post-1989

Stephenson, James. *Losing the Golden Hour: An Insider's View of Iraq's Reconstruction.* Washington: Potomac Books, 2007. A vivid account by the 2004–5 USAID mission director, a Foreign Service officer expert in post-conflict transition, of what it was like to live and work in war-torn Iraq.

FOREIGN DIPLOMATIC HISTORY

Khan, Riaz. *Untying the Afghan Knot: Negotiating Soviet Withdrawal.* Durham, NC: Duke University Press, 1991. An authoritative insider's account by the senior Pakistani diplomat involved in the eight-year negotiations among all the major players leading to the 1988 Geneva Accords.

DIPLOMATIC MEMOIRS AND BIOGRAPHIES

Grove, Brandon. *Behind Embassy Walls: The Life and Times of an American Diplomat.* Columbia: University of Missouri Press, 2005. A highly literate account of a thirty-five-year diplomatic career in Africa, Europe, Central America, and the Middle East.

Kennan, George. *Memoirs 1925-1950.* New York: Random House, 1983. This book by one of America's most influential diplomats brings to life major events of U.S. diplomatic history of his era.

Spain, James W. *In Those Days: A Diplomat Remembers.* Kent, OH: Kent State University Press, 1998. A diplomatic life on the edge, told with a bluntness leavened with feeling and humor, by a career diplomat and four-time ambassador, to Tanzania, Turkey, Sri Lanka, and the United Nations.

DIPLOMATIC CUSTOMS, ETIQUETTE, AND LIFE

Bender, Margaret. *Foreign at Home and Away: Foreign-born Wives in the U.S. Foreign Service.* Writers Club Press, 2002. Individual stories of Foreign Service life interwoven with themes such as transitions, work, children, senior wives, CIA wives, marital problems, post–Foreign Service life, and home country reentry.

Feltham, R. G., *Diplomatic Handbook.* 7th ed. London/New York: Longman, 1998. A practical guide for managers of diplomatic practice.

Linderman, Patricia, and Melissa Brayer Hess, eds. *Realities of Foreign Service Life.* San Jose, CA: Writers Club Press, 2002. An honest and balanced view of the realities of life in the Foreign Service.

DIPLOMACY THEORY AND PRACTICE

Berridge, G. R. *Diplomacy: Theory and Practice.* 4th ed. Basingstoke, UK: Palgrave-Macmillan, 2010. An up-to-date treatment of foreign ministries, the art of negotiation, and modes of diplomacy by a leading scholar.

Berridge, G. R., and Alan James. *A Dictionary of Diplomacy.* 2nd ed. Basingstoke, UK: Palgrave Macmillan, 2004. A comprehensive guide to all aspects of diplomacy, continually updated online.

Cohen, Raymond. *Negotiating across Cultures: Communications Obstacles in U.S. Diplomacy.* Washington: U.S. Institute of Peace, 1991. An astute diplomatic scholar examines the ways cultural factors have affected U.S. dealings with Japan, China, Egypt, India, and Mexico over forty years.

Dorman, Shawn, ed. *Inside a U.S. Embassy: Diplomacy at Work.* Washington: American Foreign Service Association/Potomac Books, 2011. Details the inner workings of U.S. embassies around the globe, including firsthand accounts of diplomacy in action.

Freeman, Chas. *Arts of Power: Statecraft and Diplomacy.* Washington: U.S. Institute of Peace, 1997. A thought-provoking manual for the professional diplomat that provides an outline and introduction to diplomatic thought and practice.

Miller, Robert Hopkins et al. *Inside an Embassy: The Political Role of Diplomats Abroad.* Washington: Congressional Quarterly Books, 1992. How diplomats carry out embassy political functions, with cases and illustrative political reporting.

Nicolson, Harold. *Diplomacy.* New York: Harcourt Brace, 1939. A classic work that explores the origins of diplomacy, its development, basic diplomatic practices, and the personal qualities required of successful diplomats.

Nye, Joseph. *Soft Power: The Means to Success in World Politics.* New York: Public Affairs, 2004. Makes the case for using the "soft power" of U.S. public diplomacy aboard.

Tuch, Hans N. *Communicating with the World: U.S. Public Diplomacy Overseas.* New York: St. Martin's, 1990. A seasoned practitioner vividly explains how diplomatic missions abroad practice public diplomacy.

AREA STUDIES

Africa

Cohen, Herman J. *Intervening in Africa: Superpower Peacemaking in a Troubled Continent.* Basingstoke, UK: Macmillan; New York: St. Martin's, 2000. A candid account of the 1989–93 Africa Bureau's attempts to resolve seven civil wars, with mixed results.

Hume, Cameron R. *Mission to Algiers: Diplomacy by Engagement.* Lanham, MD: Lexington Books, 2006. A firsthand account of expanding bilateral relations during Algeria's partially successful transition to democracy and of an ambassador's role.

East Asia and Pacific

Platt, Nicholas. *China Boys: How U.S. Relations with the PRC Began and Grew.* Washington: New Academia, 2010. A close-up view of the U.S. opening to China and the pioneer days in relations that followed, including the forging of the first links between the Pentagon and the People's Liberation Army.

Tucker, Nancy Bernkopf, ed. *China Confidential: American Diplomats and Sino-American Relations, 1945–1996.* New York: Columbia University Press, 2001. A China scholar draws from fifty-one diplomatic oral histories to weave together inside views of how American policy toward China has been made over the last seven decades.

Europe and Eurasia

Smith, Raymond F. *Negotiating with the Soviets.* Bloomington: Indiana University Press, 1989. A diplomat with extensive experience in bilateral relations with Moscow analyzes underlying patterns of Russian political behavior and negotiating conduct, with many vivid examples and still timely insights.

Near East

Hart, Parker T. *Saudi Arabia and the United States: Birth of a Security Partnership.* **Bloomington: Indiana University Press, 1999.** An eyewitness account of the sometimes bumpy evolution of the critical U.S.-Saudi relationship from the 1930s through the mid-1960s.

USEFUL WEBSITES

http://memory.loc.gov/ammem/collections/diplomacy/ (oral history collection of the Association for Diplomatic Studies and Training)

www.adst.org (includes details of books in ADST's two series)

www.afsa.org (the site of the American Foreign Service Association, which represents the Foreign Service in labor negotiations with the State Department and provides a broad variety of services to its members)

www.americandiplomacy.org (*American Diplomacy* online journal)

www.state.gov/r/pa/ho/ (U.S. Department of State's Office of the Historian)

www.usdiplomacy.org (an exploration of diplomatic history and foreign affairs)

INDEX

NSC (National Security Council), 16, 20

objectives of political analysis, 10–14
objectivity, 2, 4, 122
Open Forum Panel, 134
oral political analysis, 4–5, 28, 39, 134
organization, 62, 81

Pakistan, 47
paradigm shifts
    as analytical tools, 49–55, 59
    bureaucracies and, 134–35
    policies and, 118–22
personality and charisma, 58–59
personal messages from ambassadors, 22, 23, 27, 130
personal paradigms, 121
personal tools. *See* tools, personal
personal views of diplomats, 3–4, 115–20, 122, 124–26, 134–35
policies
    impact of technology and bureaucracy on making, 129–130
    influences on, 12–13, 20, 32–34, 64–65, 129
    obligation of diplomat to follow, 125–126
    recommending, 12–14, 93–96, 119–22
    when diplomats' views differ, 115–16, 118–22

political analysis. *See also* reporting, political
    as a craft, 2–5
    as art, 2, 92, 135–36
    defined, 1–2, 7
political appointees, 12–13, 20, 117–18
political culture, 45, 56–58, 94, 101
political leadership and foreign policy, 20–21, 26, 30, 32, 56, 122
politics, defined, 1
Post Reporting Plans (PRPs), 51
power
    case study on Soviet, 96–101, 105, 108, 110–14
    personality and charisma, 59
    politics and, 1–2, 33, 56
    right to rule, 46–47
    structure of, 52–53
PowerPoint, 5
practitioners of political analysis, 3–4
precedence of dispatch information, 21–22
prediction
    correct usage, 9–10, 16, 35–36
    probability analysis, 54–55, 92–93
    reporting awards, 64
predictive accuracy, 64
president, functions of, 12, 20
press, 18, 31–32, 123, 125
prioritizing, 17, 21, 26, 36
probability analysis, 45, 54–55, 92–93
Putin, Vladimir, 57

ABOUT THE AUTHOR

Raymond F. Smith worked for the State Department for several decades, primarily doing political analysis, before retiring with the rank of minister counselor in the Senior Foreign Service. He held two of the most significant analytical jobs in the State Department: minister counselor for political affairs at the U.S. Embassy in Moscow, and director of the Office of Russian, Central Asian, Caucasus, and Eastern European Affairs, Bureau of Intelligence and Research. He is the author of *Negotiating with the Soviets* (Indiana University Press, 1989). He lives in Dallas.